Christians Must Choose

The Lure of Culture and the Command of Christ

Christians Must Choose
The Lure of Culture
and the Command of Christ

by Jan G. Linn

CBP Press
St. Louis, Missouri

All scripture quotations, unless otherwise indicated, are from the Revised Standard Version of the Bible, copyrighted 1946, 1952, © 1971, 1973 by the Division of Christian Education of the National Council of Churches of Christ in the United States of America, and used by permission.

Library of Congress Cataloging in Publication Data

Linn, Jan.
    Christians must choose.

    1. Christianity and culture. 2. Church renewal. 3. United States—Church history—20th century.
    I. Title.
BR115.C8L56   1985   277.3'0828   85-3731
ISBN 0-8272-0448-5

Manufactured in the United States of America

For

Ronald Osborn

who has taught so many of us
what it means to do ministry
in Christ's place

Foreword

The late William Temple, archbishop of Canterbury, put many of us in his debt by his frequent utterances about Christian renewal. Far from being a mere adjunct to the Christian cause, Temple saw renewal as integral and potentially eternal. Indeed, he took seriously the proposition of the gospel which affirms that the powers of death will not prevail. Perhaps Temple's most unforgettable sentence is: "The supreme wonder of the history of the Christian Church is that always in the moments when it has seemed most dead, out of its own body there has sprung up new life." Renewal, indeed, comes normally, not from any external pressure, but from within the fellowship itself. The wonder is not merely that of renewal, even in dark times, but of self-renewal. My friend, Jan Linn, is one who undertands this.

I have watched Jan Linn for several years and am always grateful for the fact that in his student days he visited me in my library on the campus of Earlham College. I have encouraged him to write for publication, convinced that his message is one which the world needs. I hope that what he has written will attract many readers, including those who have been perplexed about the validity of the Christian mission. Fortunately, Jan Linn has no doubt about his position in this connection.

My hope is that some who read this book will recognize, perhaps for the first time in their lives, that they are called, not merely to support renewal, but to practice it.

D. Elton Trueblood

Contents

Acknowledgements

This book has had a lot of help along the way, although its shortcomings are solely my own. The members of the Adult Class at St. John's Episcopal Church in Lynchburg faithfully attended several lectures on this material in its formative stages. They have made a habit of providing me a forum to share ideas stirring around in my head and heart, for which I am deeply grateful.

Betty Hempfling and Wilbur Ressler read very early drafts of some of the chapters and encouraged me to continue the work. Many of my students and colleagues also encouraged this effort, sometimes without realizing it, through small group discussions and personal conversations.

At a critical point, a trusted friend, Bill McGraw, helped me clarify material in the last chapter, providing fresh direction for the entire book. His insights made it possible for me to get beyond a period in which I was unable to focus my thoughts.

I am indebted to a group of ministerial colleagues whose constructive suggestions helped make this a better book than it otherwise would be: Leroy Ashworth, Fred Helsabeck, Joe Robinson, Jr., Jim Bishop, Bob Bohannon, Bill Porter, Norman West, Bob Spaulding, and Carolyn Higginbotham.

I am also grateful to Lynchburg College for allowing me to be a member of a community that not only supports the free exchange of ideas, but also provides time for putting them in written form.

My deepest gratitude goes to my secretary, Mrs. Lucille Ferrell, for her matchless skill and patience in typing, and in concealing the fact that I actually work for her; and to my wife,

Delores, who possesses the insight of an editor, which has often been quite humbling.

Finally, a special word of appreciation needs to be expressed to Dr. Elton Trueblood for consenting to write the Foreword, especially for doing this during the difficult period of the loss of his wife, Virginia. I count it a genuine privilege to be among those whose lives have been significantly shaped by his influence.

Jan Linn
Lynchburg College
Spring 1985

Introduction

It is now clear that for mainline Protestant churches in America, the 1980s is a time for renewed emphasis on evangelism. Almost with one voice, clergy and laity are calling for greater evangelistic zeal. Denominations are launching new programs in evangelism.[1] Workshops on evangelistic methods have proliferated in the last few years.

This concern stems in part from a belief that evangelism is the primary responsibility of the church. Even more, it is a response to the sagging life our churches are experiencing. It is noteworthy that this emphasis on evangelism is coming at a time when attendance and income are down across the board. Many people believe that the last decade was a period when churches did not do much about evangelism, and the present decline is the result. They cite growing churches that emphasize evangelism as proof for their point of view.

But evangelism is not a cure for sagging church life. It never has been, as past efforts should have proven.[2] This is because the need for evangelism and the need for new vitality in the church are two very different concerns. *Evangelism* focuses on conversion; *renewal* focuses on faithfulness. Both are important. But to think evangelism can solve the problem of a declining church is like sending new troops to turn the tide of a losing battle when the real problem lies in not understanding the nature of the fight.

It is not surprising that evangelism is being used as a way to bring new life to churches. In a significant way it is a sign of the times. It reflects the kind of "quick fix" and "immediate satisfaction" society we live in. It can bring tangible results in a short period of time. This is especially appealing in light of the Great Commission Jesus has given to us (*Matthew 28:18-20*).

Yet a quick fix is never a suitable solution to a long-term problem. We are beginning to understand this in regard to our economy. I believe that as Christians we need to realize the same thing is true for the church. We must go beyond evangelism and confront a much more fundamental problem that is the real cause of sagging church life. That problem is *enculturation.*

Enculturation of the church refers to that condition in which churches compromise their faithfulness to Christ by *allowing the values of the surrounding culture to dominate their beliefs and practices.*[3] It is my conviction that enculturation, not the lack of evangelism, is the cause of church anemia. It has blurred our vision of what it means to be church and to do ministry. This is because it drives a wedge between the church and Christ. As long as we do nothing to break out of our cultural bondage, our best efforts in evangelism will be little more than taking an aspirin for a fever while ignoring the infection that is causing the problem.

Not only is evangelism not enough to cope with enculturation, but it actually makes the problem worse, though not by intention. It brings new converts into churches already engulfed in enculturation. Soon the new members become like the rest of us. They begin thinking and believing and acting in enculturated ways. And, like the rest of us, they do so without even realizing what has happened to them. Thus, inadvertently, evangelism often serves to undercut itself. Conversion leads to enculturation, which causes unfaithfulness, which in turn weakens the original conversion. (There is also the problem of evangelistic methods themselves becoming enculturated, something discussed in chapter 2.)

What, then, should we do? Call for a moratorium on evangelism? Hardly. Not only would such a call be ignored, it is not even consistent with the true nature of the Christian faith (see chapter 5). What we can do is recognize what enculturation is doing to us and take the first steps necessary to limit its influence on us.

That, however, is something you don't want to do. At least that is what some church leaders think. In conversations about evangelism and enculturation, they have told me that you, the laity, don't want to hear what's wrong with the church. You want to accentuate the positive. "Possibility thinking" is in! In surveying the books currently on the market, publishers apparently agree.

I think that this point of view sells you short. I would argue that it misjudges what you think and believe about the church, and what you are willing to read and discuss. It certainly does not reflect the attitude of hundreds of lay people (and not a few clergy) I have met in the last few years. The encouragement to put this material into book form has come from them. They are not naive about the problems their congregations are experiencing. They may want to hear good things about the church. They may believe evangelism is important. But they are also anxious to know what can be done to help people like themselves who are already church members. Many of them feel that they have been forgotten. They want to be fed and nurtured, and they don't want pablum! This book seeks to respond to them.

Perhaps at this point I should emphasize that this is not a book written against evangelism. Saying evangelism is not enough does not mean it is unimportant. Evangelism is not the problem. Rather, the problem is in what many people believe evangelism is and what they think it can do for churches.

In this discussion, the emphasis *is* on the positive. Our focus is not on the problem of enculturation but on its solutions. We face a great challenge. At stake are both the validity and credibility of the life and witnesses of the churches in America. It is possible that we are living at a time when the choices we make will change the course of events in church history.

But we can meet this challenge. To do so, however, we need what the American journalist and scholar, Max Lerner, calls "tough-mindedness."[4] This means having the will to see reality as it is. Lerner contrasts "tough-mindedness" with what he calls "soft-mindedness," which is seeing reality as we want it to be rather than the way it really is.

You are invited to become a "tough-minded" Christian. This is an invitation to believe in the future of the church, not because of confidence in the present state of the church's health but because of the firm conviction that God has always given his people the strength to renew their covenantal vows when they have turned back to God. Becoming "tough-minded" means we will be choosing life over death, faithfulness over apostasy, Christ over culture. This is the challenge this book attempts to set forth.

1

The Cultural Bondage of the Church

We have already defined enculturation. It symbolizes the inability of congregations to know how to be *in* the world but not *of* it. Societal values have slowly infected church life to the point where our identity is confused and our mission is unsure. The situation is not hopeless, but anyone who does not think it is serious does not know what is happening to the church.

It is my conviction that enculturation is not only weakening church life, but also is producing a crisis of faith. What we are faced with is a challenge to the validity of what we believe. The dominance of societal values in church life makes real the issue of whether or not we really believe God exists. We will have to answer some important questions if we want to face up to what enculturation is doing to us. If we believe God exists, does his will make any practical difference in the way churches make their decisions or conduct their work? Do churches live in such a way that we proclaim that Jesus' life, death, and resurrection marked the dawn of a new age of values and authority? Those questions cannot be ignored, and we cannot assume the answers to be obvious. Enculturation is testing all our talk about the transcendent nature of church life.

But at this point you may be naturally questioning why I believe church life is suffering under cultural bondage. Is there any sound basis for this conclusion? Let me describe some churches I know. Then let me identify the way(s) I think they are showing signs of enculturation. In the next chapter we will expand our analysis of enculturation's effect, and suggest steps that need to be taken to curb its influence. For now, ask yourself whether or not these signs sound familiar. It will be interesting to know whether or not any of these descriptions fit your congregation.

Congregation #1

Description: This is a large congregation in a changing neighborhood. Weekly Sunday school and worship attendance average over 500, with a membership that exceeds 1200. The congregation is predominantly blue collar. They are a generous and loving people who depend heavily on professional leadership for guidance. They are conservative theologically but are not closed minded. Change is painful for them. They sing gospel hymns and still hold annual revivals (week-long preaching services).

Some other facts are important to know about this congregation. Generous financial giving has led the leadership to build a savings account of over $180,000. In the last few years, overall attendance has declined significantly, although the church continues to receive new members each year. The majority of the members think that their church is in decline. The majority would also say that the lack of effective evangelistic programming is the primary cause of this decline. Finally, social ministries have been a source of controversy when the annual budget has been written. More than 90 percent of the income is spent on themselves; less than 10 percent is given to all the outreach programs combined.

Analysis: This congregation has become a victim of enculturation in several ways. One, the members have accepted the American value *"bigger is better."* They believe that *numbers* are not only a reliable but also the primary indicator of the health of their congregation. Most of their promotional appeal is directed at increasing attendance. On special occasions such as Rally Day and Easter, attendance goals are set for each Sunday school class.

The members' concern for attendance has its roots in a genuine concern for evangelism. But they have equated evangelism with church growth. This means evangelism has only one form in this church—visitation programs and promotional appeal. They do not understand social ministries, educational programs, or foreign mission support as evangelism.

By equating church growth with evangelism, this congregation has become the victim of societal business standards in a way that distorts the biblical meaning of evangelism. The members have accepted the notion that growth means faithfulness to the Great Commission (*Matthew 28:8-20*). For them, growth is a sign of a successful church. What is worse, their evangelism has been consciously segregated. While the church is in an integrated neighborhood, its evangelistic callers have been careful to avoid black families.

Another sign of enculturation in this congregation is their effort to secure their own future with a savings account. They think the money they have in savings is there to protect them against a financial crises. This may make good business sense, but it is difficult to see how it squares with the life of the Lord of the church, the One who did not have anywhere even to lay his head (*Matthew 8:20*). One wonders what has happened to the members' belief in God as one who provides daily for his people (*Numbers 11:7-9, 31-32; Matthew 6:25-34*).

This sign of enculturation also contradicts the clear call Jesus gave to the church to care for the poor, the sick, the imprisoned, and the forgotten (*Matthew 25:31-46*). Jesus went so far as to say, in this parable, that the way we will be finally judged will be the way we have treated such people. With the poor of the world—and even America—growing in numbers, and those who are already poor getting poorer,[5] the extent to which enculturation has blurred this congregation's understanding of faithful discipleship seems obvious. Where is the outrage these Christians should be feeling over the suffering of the poor? Where is their desire to be identified with them? Has enculturation convinced them they can worship God in spirit and truth while separating themselves from the kind of people with whom Jesus spent most of his ministry?

Now, it is important to keep in mind that the members of this congregation are people like you and me. They are sincere in their intentions to live as Christians. They support their church with regular attendance and giving. But their sincerity has not exempted them from the effects of enculturation that is eroding the foundations of their life together.

Congregation #2
Description: This congregation is a small one in a small town.

17

The members are well educated, predominantly professional, but aging. There are few young couples with small children.

The worship life is very liturgical. It is the center of congregational activity. The Lectionary is followed, with emphasis on special holy days. The members take pride in their church. They also want to be proud of their minister and family in the community at large. Thus a certain amount of social sophistication is expected of them.

This congregation is over 100 years old. It has had, and continues to have, several very wealthy members who have been generous in their financial support. At this point in their history they have accumulated assets in savings, stocks, and bonds in excess of a million dollars. This money has recently been set aside to provide a permanent endowment for the congregation. The financial future is secure, even if no one ever gave another dollar to the church.

Theologically the congregation is moderate to liberal, although politically very conservative. Social ministries are not supported to the extent they could be, but such support is not a matter of controversy. In addition, scholarship funds for those entering full-time ministry as well as for those going into other professions have been established for young people within and outside the congregation.

Analysis: There are similarities and similar signs of enculteration between this congregation and congregation #1. But one additional sign stands out. It is *institutional perpetuation.* The members of this church have been concerned to secure its future. This is the reason for the endowment funds. Being small in a small town, the congregation's numerical growth has always been limited. Those concerned about the church have thought the best way to show their concern was through endowment funds. This way, the church's future would always be secure.

Here again, it seems enculturation has distorted the members' understanding of the nature of the church and its future. They have failed either to realize or believe that the future belongs to God and cannot be secured by us. We can endow a societal institution, but we cannot endow the church's future. That future is always a gift of God's grace.

This is precisely what the story of Abraham's willingness to sacrifice Isaac makes clear (*Genesis 22:1-14*). When Abraham laid Isaac on the altar, the future of Israel was hanging in the balance. A knife in Isaac would have killed the anticipated and promised future. Isaac was the designated heir. But Abraham risked obedience over security, and he discovered the paradox that security for the people of God lies in the will to risk everything to follow God's will.

It should be clear to us that institutional perpetuation is a cultural value that has no place in the church. It contradicts the very nature of biblical faith. It leads the church not only to misuse its financial resources but also to play it safe in ministry. It blunts our will to follow Christ to the point of death and weakens trust in God as One who has power to bring forth new life, even from the tomb. Institutional perpetuation makes getting involved in controversial issues a dangerous game to play. Controversy is one thing institutions seeking to secure their future must avoid. This means that in the church, prophetic voices are unwelcome. Prophets stir things up. They talk about controversial issues and make people uncomfortable.

The question the members of this congregation need to answer is how they understand the prophetic call that ministry always includes. They should carefully study what happened to the official church of Germany during the Hitler years. No generation of Christians can afford to ignore the implications of the comment of Joseph Goebbels, Hitler's Minister of Propaganda, when he said to a group of church leaders, "You are free to seek your salvation, provided you do nothing to change the social order."

Again, it is important to remember that these church members are as sincere as the rest of us. They are not intentionally undercutting the very ministry they are seeking to fulfill. Unfortunately, at this point, they simply do not seem to realize what they are doing to themselves.

Congregation #3

Description: This congregation is a medium-sized church with an average weekly attendance for Sunday worship of 200. It is made up of blue-collar workers and young professionals, the latter being the more dominant group in terms of congregational leadership. It is a fairly homogeneous congregation, even in its diversity. The people pride themselves on how well they get along with one another. They are also proud of the fact that they are a "middle-aged" and younger congregation. They see their future as a bright one.

A smoothly running, functional committee type of organization characterizes this congregation. Members are elected to serve on the various committees annually. A rotating board of elders and deacons form the decision-making body of the church, with both men and women serving in both capacities.

Theologically, the people are moderate to conservative. They support social ministries, though not without objections from some of the members. They believe in a well-educated and highly skilled professional leadership. They strongly support denominational identification. Some of their members serve on denominational commissions and boards.

On the surface, things seem to be going well. Yet the minister is very frustrated because the members see what they do as supporting his ministry. From his perspective, they have a limited understanding of their ministries, giving themselves to a point but then backing away.

He is also frustrated by the fact that they do not show any interest in serious Christian education. The adult program is dominated by a large young adult class that doesn't do much more on Sunday mornings than deal superficially with topics. The members resist starting the class at an earlier hour in order to have more time for study. They have also rejected spending any extended period of time studying a subject in depth, such as a book in the Bible or an important contemporary issue. The minister has reached the conclusion that about all they come to Sunday School for is to see one another. While he agrees that fellowship is important, he believes serious study also needs to be a part of their time together. But he has not had much success in getting them to make the changes necessary for this to happen.

Analysis: The primary problem with this congregation is that the members are perpetuating *"mild religion,"* one of the most troublesome influences of enculturation.[6] Yet they are probably not really conscious of how "mild" their commitment is because they are active in the organizational program of their church.

What has happened is that, for many members of the church, discipleship is only one among many other demands on their already busy schedules. They are full participants in mainstream America. They are upwardly mobile families, career oriented, and very success conscious. While it would be unfair to say church membership is nothing more than a social obligation to them, it is true that for many of them it has social value in their careers, even as social club memberships do.

Enculturation has convinced the members of this congregation that they can be in the church and of the world at the same time. Enculturation has tempted them to compromise the radical nature of the teachings of Jesus by reinterpreting them to fit the modern age with its many demands and opportunities. It is reasonable to assume that they understand Christian ethics as having to be rooted in a realistic view of how the world is run, how things get done, and how people get ahead.

At the same time, these church members are extremely talented. The church needs their abilities for leadership and witness. But enculturation blocks the church from ever really reaching these people. They belong to the church, but many of them do not belong to Christ. They follow him at a safe distance. Jesus is more of a person of history than the living Lord of their lives. To a significant degree, the church has their head, but culture has their heart.

Congregation #4

Description: This is an exceptionally large church, having several thousand members. It is ultraconservative and fundamentalistic by its own admission. It has a radio and television ministry. The minister and the members say they believe God has commissioned them to save the soul of America. Their primary goal is "soul winning." Salvation is a private matter between a person and God. They believe there is an urgency about "soul winning" that often leads them to ignore a person's right to privacy and freedom from religious coercion or harassment.

The members of this congregation are radical anticommunists. They view communism as the seedbed for the antichrist, as a godless system that is gradually spreading through the world like a cancer. For them, America is an especially blessed nation with a divine mission to save the world from communism. They wear "Jesus First" pins and American flags on their coat lapels.[7] Moreover, they believe that capitalism best suits the survival-of-the-fittest kind of society in which they fervently believe. In their view, welfare is basically parasitic.

Analysis: This congregation shows several of the signs of enculturation already discussed. But two additional ones should be noted. The first is the Americanization of the *gospel.* What this means is that they have welded the gospel to American nationalism, convincing themselves that loyalty to God and country are two sides of the same coin. For them patriotism and discipleship have become synonymous.[8] They have wrapped the American flag around the Bible without seeing any danger in doing so. At times they seem to be more concerned about being loyal Americans than loyal Christians.

The second sign of enculturation this congregation demonstrates is closely related to Americanization of the gospel. It is the *privatization of faith.* They have gone beyond the personal gospel and have made a person's relationship to God a private matter. The popular song of a few years ago entitled "Me and Jesus Got Our Own Thing Going" aptly describes the way these church members understand their faith.

Privatization of faith has led these people to a radical concern for the fate of people's souls. They have spiritualized the gospel to mean "soul winning." It is no surprise that these Christians show a paucity of concern for and involvement in social ministries.

One wonders if these church members realize that limiting the sovereignty of God to a concern for spiritual matters amounts to idolatry. It eliminates the social and political dimensions of God's involvement in history that the prophets and Jesus clearly underscored as central. This is an insidious form of enculturation that robs the church of integrity. Moreover, it particularly characterizes American church life today.

Congregation #5

Description: This congregation is extremely small. In fact, it is barely hanging on, with about 50 active members. It has limited financial resources and cannot compete against larger churches for qualified professional leadership. The average age of the members is around 55 to 60. They have trouble attracting young couples because they are so small and old, yet they are small and old because they cannot attract young couples. They are caught in a circle from which there seems to be no escape.

The members of this congregation are also gracious and loving. They are both blue-collar and professional, college graduates and noncollege persons. They love their little church. Many of them have been in it all their lives, going back two or three generations. They are faithful in attendance and generous in giving.

But they are discouraged about their church. They have a limited view of what they are able to do as a congregation. Long-time survival is a legitimate question in their minds. They see themselves as basically hanging on, able only to attract limited ministerial leadership. They go through the motions without much life in what they are doing.

Analysis: This congregation suffers from having accepted the cultural value that power is in size. They have become discouraged as the years have seen them grow smaller and smaller, giving in to the enculturated notion that they are not worth much in their denomination, that they are too small to make much difference or to matter very much.

Describing this church is important in our discussion because it is one of the saddest situations in church life today. Enculturation, often perpetuated by the denomination of which they are a part, has caused them to forget that, in the Bible, power in the church comes from Christ, not from us. The way we make contact with that power is through commitment. They need to hear the stories of how small groups of committed Christians have made significant impacts on their communities.[9] They also need to be shown that small committed groups are more powerful than large groups in which part of the membership has only halfhearted commitment.

There are many churches like this one in all denominations. Their ministries are wasting away because of the effect enculturation is having on them. The gifts for ministry Christ gives to his church (*1 Cor. 12-13; Eph. 4:11-16*) have been given to all churches, not simply to large ones. The members of these churches need to know that how society defines power is not the way it is in the kingdom of God.

These examples of enculturated churches are actual congregations. They are a microscopic view of what exists in varying degrees in all churches. Enculturation is a disease that is draining life from our churches in such a gradual way that its signs are not obviously discernible. This may be because all areas of our lives are pervaded by the surrounding culture. It is not easy to recognize that which totally surrounds and influences our life.

A Covenant People

One of the reasons church life has become enculturated to the extent it has lies in the fact that as members we have forgotten that we are the *b'nai b'rith,* the children of covenant, and not simply the *b'nai Elohim,* the children of God. The distinction between the two is important.

Calling ourselves the people of God reminds us of the graciousness of God and his love for all his people. But in calling ourselves the people of covenant we are reminded that we have responsibilities in this relationship. The church is made up of people who have realized their covenant responsibilities and have willingly accepted them. In Christ we have become bonded with God in such a way that our life style marks us as belonging to his kingdom.

Enculturation, of course, weakens our commitment to this covenant relationship by making the meaning of covenant fuzzy. This is what has happened to the churches we have just described and those like them. Before we begin to identify the practical things that must be done in response to our enculturated condition, it is well that we spend some time reviewing the meaning of covenant in the biblical tradition. To do so we can use the covenant renewal ceremonies found in the book of *Joshua* as our point of entry.

The covenant renewal ceremonies Joshua held in the vale of Shechem were pivotal experiences for Israel.[10] At Shechem the people had to choose whether they would serve Yahweh or the pagan gods of Canaanite culture. According to the Torah story, their decision would determine the future of Israel as the people of covenant. Herein is the reason why their experience can be instructive for us.

Shechem was an ancient city the Israelites had taken over when they entered the land. Jacob had bought a portion of land from the Hivites, who inhabited Shechem, when he returned to make peace with his brother, Esau (*Genesis 33:18-19*). The city was bounded by Mt. Ebal to the north and Mt. Gerizim to the south. It was on Mt. Ebal that Joshua, following the instruction of Moses, built "an altar of unhewn stones, upon which no man has lifted an iron tool" (*Joshua 8:30-31*). Here he "wrote upon the stones a copy of the law of Moses, which he had written" (*v. 32*). Afterwards, Joshua read the entire covenant law to the people (*v. 34*). Finally, it was in his farewell address (*Joshua 24*) that Joshua gathered the people once again at Shechem to renew their covenantal vows.

Several features of these renewal ceremonies define the essential elements necessary for God's covenant renewal. One is covenant renewal itself. Renewing the covenant was a time for remembrance and reevaluation for the entire community. It was a sign of the need for the people to take the time once again publicly to affirm their desire to serve God. This was not the first such renewal ceremony, according to the Torah story. Moses held one before his death (*Deuteronomy 1:3*). Nor was it the last. Ezra read the Torah from early morning until noon when the exiles returned from Babylon (*Nehemiah 8:2-3*). Covenant renewal was central to Israel's worship. This tradition continues even today. *Rosh Hashanah,* the Jewish new year, is a time for sober reexamination of the community's commitment to living by sacred covenant. We shall say more about the need for Christians to hold an annual covenant renewal ceremony in the next chapter. The important point is the place this tradition has held in the life of God's people.

A second feature about covenant renewal is its affirmation of the absoluteness of God's sovereignty. Joshua acknowledged the people's freedom to serve gods of the surrounding culture. But he made clear that doing so meant the rejection of the sovereignty of Yahweh. The First Commandment had established that covenant depended upon acknowledging the absoluteness of God's sovereignty. There were to be no other gods equal to Yahweh, and thus, no other gods to whom devotion could be given (*Exodus 20:3*).

The significance of rejecting the absoluteness of God's sovereignty was that it was symptomatic of idolatry. For Israel to turn away from worshiping Yahweh would mean she had begun to worship other gods. Idolatry destroys the basis for covenant. Jesus echoed the basis for covenant when he said:

> No one can serve two masters, for
> either he will hate the one and love
> the other, or he will be devoted to
> the one and despise the other
> (*Matthew 6:24*).

It is not only the nature of a covenant with God that requires his people to accept his absolute sovereignty. It is also its wisdom. Covenant is not possible without it. Acceptance of God's sovereignty means reliance upon his covenantal presence. It creates the expectation of his guidance and care that causes his people to look to him. He is able to sustain them both in life and spirit, making it possible for them to live by covenant.

This was a lesson the Israelites did not learn quickly. The idolatry of both Egypt and Canaan were being challenged by Joshua. Those who had traveled with him were still under the influence of Pharoah's ways. Much of their journey had been spent forgetting the oppression of their slavery and remembering its security. In Egypt, at least they knew where their next meal was coming from. They had lived in Pharoah's land long enough (400 years) to recognize the benefits of its culture, which overshadowed its idolatry. Joshua called upon them to decide if they preferred Pharoah to Yahweh.

But he also spoke to the descendants of Abraham who had not gone to Egypt. A segment of the people had stayed in Canaan, not going down to Egypt with Jacob and his clan.[11] At Shechem, Joshua asked them to give up their Canaanite ways and to recommit themselves to the covenant with Yahweh. Old habits are, of course, difficult to break. Though the people agreed to renew their covenantal vows then, they often allowed themselves to be influenced more by the values of Canaanite culture than by the commandments of the covenant. Thus, the absoluteness of God's sovereignty was always in tension with Israelite ways, as it continues to be for us as well.

A third feature of covenant renewal to notice is that it

reaffirmed identity. The Israelites were the people of Yahweh because of the covenant. This was their peculiar identity that set them apart from other people. Their wandering in the wilderness came to an end not only because they finally conquered the land. It ended when their identity as God's people was clearly established in their own minds. Had they not renewed the covenant, they could have gone into the land yet continued to wander. Identity is crucial to establishing roots. Not to know who one is-is to wander endlessly. Renewing the covenant meant reestablishing identity. Clarifying our identity today as God's people is no less important than it was for them.

Finally, covenant renewal meant defining life style. Identity and life style always go together. But life style not only expresses identity, it also shapes it. Covenantal laws were to be followed because doing so maintained identity. To forsake the life style they were to live, as defined by covenant, meant the Israelites would lose their peculiar identity. They would assimilate into the surrounding culture and cease to be Yahweh's people.

Of course, this is precisely what happened during the time of the prophets. The people continued to worship God in the temple ceremony, but their inward commitment faltered. Their ways betrayed their covenantal vows and eventually destroyed their identity. After the fall of Samaria to the Assyrians in 722 B. C., the ten tribes of the northern kingdom lost their identity completely because of assimilation. On the other hand, the remnant of Judah maintained their identity in Babylon only because they lived by the covenant.

When Joshua gathered the people at Shechem, he was calling them to a covenant of deeds and not just words, to a lifestyle and not to ceremony alone. Herein lies the ultimate lesson for us.

When each of these elements of covenant burns vividly in the minds *and* hearts of those of us who are people of covenant, there is always hope for renewed life in the church. But enculturation causes them to fade from memory, and this makes us even more susceptible to its influence. The danger this poses lies in the fact that the primary responsibility our churches have is to be a faithful covenant partner. If we are not, then nothing else really matters in church life.

Underscoring the fact that we are the *b'nai b'rith,* the children of covenant, and not only the *b'nai Elohim,* the children of God, we are ready to begin confronting the practical steps that now must be taken in any congregation that wants to be freed from cultural bondage.

2
Stepping into the Water

A Jewish Midrash has it that nothing happened at the Red Sea until an old Israelite man stepped into the water. Only then did the seas part. Another says that only after the people had gone into the sea up to their very nostrils did the waters divide and expose dry ground.

There are times when *taking a step forward* paves the way for other things to happen. The converse is also true: *Not* taking the necessary step means nothing else will happen either. Both of these propositions bear heeding by the modern church. Talking about breaking free from enculturation will not make it happen. Even praying about it will not make it happen, as important as prayer is. The Midrash describes God's response to Moses' prayer for deliverance in *Exodus 14:15* as the Egyptians pursued them as follows: "Moses, your children are in distress, the sea is barring the way while the enemy is pursuing, and you stand there and recite long prayers." Then it adds: "Thus Rabbi Eliezer used to say: 'There is a time to shorten and a time to lengthen prayer.'"

This is a time for shortened prayers in our churches. There are some steps we need to take to begin breaking free from enculturation. Refocusing our identity and clarifying our mission will not happen without decisive action on our part. By now I hope that I have convinced you that the stakes are too high for us to do nothing.

In this chapter I want to suggest what some of these steps need to be. The list will not be exhaustive, but I hope it will be suggestive and even provocative. These suggestions seek to describe a vision of the church that originates in the biblical tradition of the people of God, a people who form "the alternative community" to the culture in which they live.[12]

Recapturing vision requires some rather practical steps for the church to set its house in order. In taking these steps, we will discover the phenomenon that actions can affect thinking, as well as the other way around. Changing one's behavior can bring significant changes in one's mind and heart. Psychologist Hobart Mowrer once cited an aphorism by E. Stanley Jones in making this point: "It is easier to *act* yourself into a new way of thinking than to *think* yourself into a new way of acting."[13] While Mowrer acknowledged the value of the normal interplay of thought and action (theologically, spirit and behavior), he argued that major decisions for changing one's life style should be recognized as an important means of altering a person's attitude. He summarized his argument as follows:

The point I want to make is this. Mere thinking, talking, analyzing will not save us; our final redemption can only be found in a radically changed life style.

Then he added:

The capacity to make such a change is often dependent at least to some extent, upon new visions, new conceptions which we acquire intellectually.[14]

The Bible is filled with descriptions of the vision for the alternative community God calls his people to form. The Decalogue was that vision for Moses and Joshua. The prophet Micah described the vision when he declared:

He has showed you, O man, what is good;
and what does the Lord require of you
but to do justice, and to love kindness,
and to walk humbly with your God? (*Micah 6:8*).

Jesus made the vision clear in the Sermon on the Mount and in his challenge that all would-be disciples deny themselves, pick up the cross, and only then follow him (*Mark 8:34*).

These descriptions of the vision offer us graphic pictures of the quality of life and the nature of ministry that church life should embody. But in following the vision we must, in a manner of speaking, move from the abstract to the concrete. The following suggestions have this as their particular goal. They identify ways the church can take some immediate practical steps in coping with enculturation.

Step One: Zero Budgeting

In chapter 1 we suggested that the church's attitude toward and use of money was a sign of enculturation. One way of breaking free from this form of cultural bondage is to commit ourselves to annual zero budgeting. Very simply, this means congregations would begin each new fiscal year with a zero balance. All monies from the previous year would be spent (it is hoped in responsible ways), with no money carried from one year to the next.

Why is this step important? Because it is a practical way by which to test whether or not we mean it when we say that the church's life is dependent upon God. Zero budgeting challenges congregations to do ministry by faith, rather than depending upon financial reserves to carry them through difficult periods. Cash flow needs notwithstanding, zero budgeting offers church members a practical process wherein our words, by fiscal necessity, will have to be followed by deeds. If the members of a congregation assume shared financial responsibility for their ministry together, cash flow will not be a problem. If they do not, there will be; and this will serve as a sobering indicator of the quality of that congregation's spiritual life.

If, however, zero budgeting is to be taken seriously, another factor must be considered. This is the fact that ministry must not be determined by budget. It has to be just the opposite. That is, budgets should be determined by ministry. Congregations should first seek to understand what they honestly sense God leading them to do in ministry. Only then should a budget be considered. Enculturation tempts church members to make ministries fit budgets, which essentially pushes God out of the picture. Reversing this process can mean a significant break from this type of enculturated thinking. Had Moses taken the time to consider whether or not his congregation had the resources to make the journey from Egypt to Canaan, he never would have left Egypt. Instead, he knew that he and his company would be dependent upon God to show them both the way and the resources for the trip. The manna, we should recall, had to be gathered fresh every morning (*Exodus 16:19*). Nothing could be gathered in advance, a lesson some of the people learned the hard way (*16:20-21*).

Zero budgeting, combined with a commitment to let ministry determine budgets, is one of the ways modern church members can gather daily bread fresh every morning. Projections of income may perhaps serve as guides but should never have the final word, precisely because they cannot anticipate the unexpected ways God often provides for ministries.

Step Two: Divestment

Closely related to zero budgeting is the need for congregations to divest themselves of investments and savings. Investments and savings are two of the most revealing signs of the extent to which the church has become culturally enslaved. They represent the degree to which the church has fashioned its life to this age (*Romans 12:2*). It is not uncommon to find congregations holding thousands of dollars in savings and investments. One wonders how pleased the Lord, who had nowhere to lay his head, is with a church that has thousands (even millions) in savings? One is hard pressed to find any biblical basis for ministry being supported by interest rather than principal. It may make good business sense to do it this way, but this practice won't wash in the kingdom of God.

We have noted the disturbing trend of endowing churches.[15] While individuals with good intentions may have initiated such endowments, this trend poses a serious threat to the church's life. It is the primary temptation that will lead the church to attempt to gain the whole world while loosing its own soul. An enculturated view would argue that endowments free congregations from the anxiety of living hand-to-mouth and also provide more money for helping others. The real truth, however, is that neither of these is the case. Endowments lock the church into supporting the status quo because the church financially profits from it. What is worse, endowments create a major shift from depending on God to depending on ourselves. This is tantamount to the usurpation of the sovereignty of God. Rather than endowments being a sign that the church has begun to do some wise planning for support of its ministry. they are symptomatic of the church's failure to understand the nature of its own ministry. The congregation that depends upon endowments for its life is a congregation that has lost its true identity as Christ's church.

Further, endowments always carry the potential of creating a selfish attachment to wealth. Money has the power to create the desire for possession of it. The more we have often has the effect of making us want more. In more than a few instances, endowments have had a very negative effect upon congregations for this very reason.

Our position is that steps must be taken to limit the negative effect of endowments. They should be avoided whenever possible. But at the least, the earnings should be used only for ministries outside the congregation's own life. In addition, congregations should educate their members to the dangers of local endowments. Monies for endowment purposes need to be directed toward larger expressions of the church's ministry, such as colleges and hospitals. What sometimes appears to be a blessing turns out to be just the opposite. Endowing local congregations is an example of enculturation, not fiscal acumen, and needs to be recognized as such now.

Step Three: Annual Covenant Renewal

If we want to take seriously our claims that church membership means discipleship, then annual recommitment can be a way to demonstrate it. Renewing our covenantal relationship with God and one another invites regular self-examination to determine where we are in these relationships. Socrates once said that the unexamined life is not worth living. A good case can be made that this statement is also applicable to Christian discipleship. Unexamined commitment is not worthy of the covenantal relationship we are supposed to have. Recommitment challenges members of the church to self-examination, not for the purpose of termination but of renewal.

An annual covenant renewal service (see Appendix) is a practical way for a congregation to reaffirm its desire to be the people of God. In such a service, those gathered make a public declaration to celebrate their life together as members of Christ's church. They also commit themselves to holding one another accountable for their ministry. At Shechem, the people pledged to serve as witnesses to their own covenantal fidelity (*Joshua 24:22*).

Once a year, congregations need to set aside a particular Sunday for publicly renewing their covenant vows. Provisions can be made to read the names of members who want to renew the commitment but are unable to attend the service. It is a simple and practical, yet powerfully binding way to bring a congregation together in a fashion similar to Joshua's Shechem renewal meetings. It is not enough to leave covenant renewal to an individual act. There is strength in corporate witness that cannot be found in individual renewal. After all, God has called a *people,* not simply individuals, to himself. The church is a community.

Here we can learn from our Jewish brothers and sisters. Jews have a wonderful sense of corporate identity. Worship in the synagogue is personal but not private. There is a clear sense in synagogue worship that a people has gathered, not a group of individuals who happen to be in the same place for private worship.

Annual covenant renewal is one of the ways Christians can build corporate identity. It can be a time when the whole body of Christ makes its commitment to be the church in a specific place. Such a service might become one of the high points in the church year. Pentecost might be an appropriate time of year for this gathering. Symbols might be used in the service that could be taken home to remind each family and person of the commitment they have made (Joshua used stones to remind the people of God's faithfulness to them in bringing them into the land (*Joshua 4:1-7).*

Step Four: Identification with Marginal People

Enculturation of the American church has separated Christians from the marginal people of our society. The hungry, thirsty, and naked do not view the church of Jesus Christ as those people who stand with them. Their perception is not without foundation. The church has joined the flight to the suburbs. Those who live on the fringes of American wealth, health, employment, and education have to come to the church for help. Seldom does the church go to them.

The church's credibility with marginal people has been severely damaged. Breaking free from enculturation requires the reestablishment of our identity with them. We must once again become friends whom they see at times other than Thanksgiving and Christmas. The Salvation Army, of course, has been able to maintain identity with these people. Big steeple, "uptown" churches, as well as downtown Salvation Armies, need to be known as friends of the poor.

Beyond the presence of Christ being revealed to us, as we will note in chapter 5, identification with marginal people by all churches will serve notice to the power brokers of modern culture that their policies are bankrupt and that their power is being challenged. The word will go forth from the churches that the many who do not share the fruits of our land and our world are no longer powerless. Now they have people, positions, and resources available to them that can end the unjust wielding of power that dominates the world.

One way churches can do this is by supporting existing programs to help marginal people. Church members need to become knowledgeable about these programs, including both their strengths and weaknesses. In this way they can provide extended support and much needed help for efforts already under way in their communities. At the same time, church members can suggest ways for programs to become more efficient. Too often we have criticized without truly caring about the people in need. Our voices will be heard when those to whom we are speaking know that we support them rather than oppose them.

Marginal people in our society need the church's voice of support. They are powerless, and in America being powerless means being voiceless. Modern power brokers, whether political or economic, do not listen to powerless people. Today's marginal people need the church to stand with them and to speak on their behalf so they will not be the forgotten ones in American corporate and political life.

Step Five: Keeping Things Small

Infatuation with "bigness" in the church has more to do with cultural bondage than with the gospel. Wanting the church to grow, if we can assume this means discipleship and not simply membership, does not necessarily support the validity of large congregations. It is possible for the church to grow while congregations remain relatively small. It is equally possible for a congregation to grow large without any significant increase in genuine discipleship.

The cultural philosophy which claims bigger is better has blurred the church's perception regarding the difference between membership and discipleship. This is the reason the disease of spectatorship is epidemic in church life today. Spectatorship exists in the church when members are not exercising their own gifts in ministry. What is more, spectatorship is inevitable in large groups. It simply cannot be avoided. Large groups do not have the dynamics to call forth the gifts of all the members, or even to care deeply for everyone. Moreover, the responsibility for spectatorship does not lie solely with the individual. It is true that some people seek an observer's seat. But this fact does not alleviate a group's responsibility for reducing the possibility of mere spectatorship wherever possible. This is especially true for the church.

What has happened in modern church life is that we have become so enculturated that we now play the percentage game. That is, we have accepted spectatorship as a fact of life, leaving us with the alternative of having to go for a percentage of those who attend church. Even here we are dealing with a percentage, since we have gone so far as to distinguish between participating and nonparticipating members, which flies in the face of the fact that a nonparticipating church member is a contradiction in terms. But we have tried to get as many of the participating members involved as is possible. It is little wonder, then, that we seek large numbers. A larger number means a larger number of people in the percentage. Thirty percent of 500 members, for example, means a larger number of active people than 30 percent of 150.

Because of enculturation, we have not understood that power is in commitment rather than numbers. Thus, a small group of fifteen committed people is more powerful than a group of thirty in which only a few are actually committed. A group whose life is hampered by spectators can never reach its potential. Spectatorship drains life away from the group.

The church needs to back away from the percentage game and move closer to membership meaning discipleship. This means that we begin to structure commitment into church life, rather than leaving it solely to the discretion of individuals.

Obviously, commitment is an individual choice, but the way we structure our life together can either hamper or nurture commitment.

What is needed is for the church to commit itself to quality rather than quantity. In turn this will require us to make a concerted effort to remain small. Despite the enculturated notion that "bigger is better," large congregations are often weak congregations. This does not mean there are no weak small congregations. But we would argue that they are weak not because of size but because they have accepted the enculturated value system which has convinced them that they are weak because they are small.

Large congregations are weak congregations because of the effect that spectatorship has on the life of the group. Spectatorship requires large amounts of time and energy to overcome it. It also discourages those who are genuinely committed to the church's life and ministry. In addition, spectators often participate at the point of decision-making. While they do not accept responsibility for ministry, they are often quite willing to cast a vote on what the ministry should be.

Once we realize that strength is not in size, we can begin to break away from our enculturated need for becoming large in membership. Congregations should become determined to remain small. At the point when they grow large, a new congregation should be formed with its own life and ministry. Those congregations which are already large need to consider the possibility of subdividing into sister communities where responsibility for each community's life and ministry is assumed by the smaller unit rather than the larger church as a whole.

Small groups which worship and serve together can also be used as a structural process for reducing the size of a congregation, along with the spectatorship that is inevitably present. Small groups are, of course, not new to the church. But in most instances they have only been extensions of enculturation rather than a challenge to it. That is, small groups have seldom been seen as miniature congregations in which responsibility for evoking and exercising gifts for ministry are a necessary part of the group's life. Therefore, they have functioned with the same basic enculturated principles which dominate the life of the congregation as a whole.

We are suggesting a different type of small group; one in which spectatorship is not acceptable. To be a member of such a group, one has to be willing to be engaged in ministry. In this kind of group everyone leads at the point of his or her gift and follows at the point of the gifts of the other members. Not only the size but also the structure of this type of group limits the possibility of spectatorship. When spectatorship is confronted, enculturation is also being confronted. To be sure, small groups will not be a simple remedy to cultural bondage, but the recognition that being small enhances quality can form the basis for some practical steps that will challenge the enculturated condition of the church.

Step Six: Covenant Evangelism

Closely related to the need for keeping things small in the church is doing evangelism in ways that are consistent with what it means to be a covenant people. That the church is called to the ministry of evangelism we have no doubt. But believing we should do evangelism does not mean that we *know how*. Earlier in our discussion we argued that enculturation has significantly affected what the church is doing in evangelism today. Now we turn our attention to what it will take for us to become truly covenanted in the church's witness in the world.

The first step is for the church to reject the idea that growth is a sign of successful evangelism. That is an enculturated concept which ignores the hard reality that, if they understand the implications of the message, proclamation of a life style symbolized by a cross may not attract large numbers of people. The church does not lack in studies telling us why people attend church and why conservative churches in America are growing while most mainline congregations are not. The problem with these studies is that they do not take into account the state of enculturation the church is experiencing. It is possible, and in many cases quite likely, that people are attending church for the wrong reasons and that conservative churches are also growing for the wrong reasons. What is more, many of these studies give tacit approval of enculturation by implying that nongrowing churches should adopt the methods of growing churches. This would be true, of course, if church growth were the point. But from a biblical perspective it is not.

If church members were to reject growth as both a goal and measurement of evangelism, the church would be taking a major step forward in freeing itself from cultural bondage. Numerical growth has no relevance to discipleship. That it does in the minds of most Christians indicates how far removed we have become from the call to faithfulness so central to the biblical tradition. The Great Commission of *Matthew 28:16-20,* in which Jesus tells his disciples to go preaching into all the world, has been allowed to overshadow everything else he said about discipleship. These verses have also become the justification for all manner of enculturated methods of church growth, from the use of fear among children to giving away awards and prizes to individuals and congregations.

The basis for thinking about evangelism in a way that is free from enculturation lies in a fresh reading of the Great Commission passage that places it within the context of the whole gospel message.

The Gospels were written from the perspective of faith as experience (see chapter 5). The Great Commission needs to be understood within this context, making it possible for us to cut through the enculturation surrounding the predominant views of evangelism. A guiding principle for nonenculturated evangelism is that the method(s) of sharing our faith must be consistant with the experiential nature of our faith. In other words, the methods of evangelism should increase the possibility of experiencing the presence of Christ. Few people would take issue with this principle, yet many of the prevailing methods do contradict the nature of the Christian experience. Thus, a review of the Great Commission is in order.

According to Matthew's theological perspective, Jesus is the new authority for Israel. He takes great care in the Mount of Transfiguration scene (*17:1-8*) to show that the primary traditions of authority in Israel (the law and the prophets) have been incorporated into the authority of Jesus. The disciples are now to listen to Jesus. The Great Commission passage begins with an affirmation of his authority. Jesus has the authority to send the disciples out to evangelize. He once called them to be with him. Now he authorizes them to go out and preach in his name.

Matthew 28:19 is usually translated, "Go . . . and make

disciples of all nations." But a more exact translation is, "Go . . . and *disciple* all the nations." The difference seems only minor, but it is actually very significant. The first translation tends to lead us into misunderstanding the role we play in evangelism. Translating Jesus' words as a commission for Christians to go make disciples creates the illusion that we can actually make someone a Christian. When we believe this, the next step is to begin measuring the effectiveness of evangelism by how many converts we make. Yet the truth is we do not make converts, and we do not make disciples. *Acts* tells us that God added to the church those who were being saved (*Acts 2:47*), which means that the power and effectiveness of evangelism lies with God and not us.

The second translation ("disciple all the nations"), on the other hand, leaves no doubt about our role in evangelism. Discipling means to teach, as Jesus further clarifies in *verse 20*. By teaching we expose others to the relationship they can have with Christ. In teaching them we are inviting them into Christ's presence. By teaching we have the chance to introduce others to Christ, which is consistent with the nature of the Christian experience itself.

But we should recognize the limitations on teaching. It does not possess the power to convert. Only the presence of Christ himself can do that. Our teaching, then, must be used by God to do his work. It has no power of its own. It is critical that we be clear about this.

Equally important for us to understand is how to teach in evangelism. There are many ways to teach, but the most effective has always been to *show* students what we want them to learn. And when it comes to the gospel, showing is more important than talking. Modeling the experience of living in Christ is the most effective method available for us to disciple other people. If we do not model what we want them to learn, nothing we say is going to make much difference in the long run. God cannot use our words if he does not first have our lives. If there is any single factor that has diminished the role we play in evangelism, it lies right here. Too often Christians have been long on talk and short on action. In the place of modeling or living the gospel we have substituted gimmicks and elaborate programs that have an emotional impact but do very little to disciple (teach) anyone. Evangelism needs to be understood as discipling—teaching—not making converts and certainly not gaining new church members. While one might hope for church growth, it must not become a goal or be used as the measuring rod for the church's fulfillment of the Great Commission.

One of the by-products of understanding evangelism this way is seeing that it has many forms. The dominant view of evangelism in the church is too narrow. Enlistment of converts is thought by most Christians to be evangelism, while social ministries, educational ministries, and even covenant renewal efforts are not. They are, so to speak, after the fact. These efforts are not understood as ways to teach discipleship.

But this is a restricted view of what Jesus' commission to "disciple" the nations means. Becoming a Christian is a realized but not yet completed experience. If Christian evangelism means becoming a disciple of Jesus, then most of us need evangelizing our entire lives. Moreover, it would seem that attracting non-Christians to Christ is more a matter of inviting them to join our journey than of finding what we have found. Conversion, after all, involves not only turning away from the world but also embracing a new life style. It is a two-step process, and both involve a lifetime of struggle and growth.[16]

It may be that the most effective evangelism in today's world is in a congregation whose members are alive with a spirit of joy and hope, yet realistic about the difficulties of living as a covenant people. This spirit is more than being warm and friendly. Being warm and friendly, as desirable as these qualities may be, does little to teach the gospel. The congregation that is genuinely alive in the faith has members who are seriously engaged in exploring the depths possible in the Christian experience. What is more, such a congregation will not have to worry about growth and survival.

Step Seven: Recovering the Model of the Pastor as Theologian[17]

Today's minister seems to be the jack-of-all-trades, and also the master of none. Local pastors are administrators, counselors, motivators, promoters, organizers, caregivers, programmers, fire fighters, and referees—all in addition to being people. What is most often lacking in the list of roles, however, is that of theologian—specifically, biblical theologian. Yet it is the call to be theologians that constitutes the essential role of the pastor.

41

Some (though not all) of the above mentioned roles may have legitimacy in the ministry, but none of them has integrity apart from the pastor being knowledgeable as a student of both the Bible and the church's traditions.

Ministry means service in the name of God; service commissioned by God; and service empowered by God. Ministry is all about God and his relationship to people and the whole of creation. The nature of ministry requires the clergy to be theologians first and last. We are those called by Christ to dare to speak about, for, and to God in the life of the church as understanding to do so is given to us.

James Armstrong, former president of the National Council of Churches, once made the statement that the most neglected resource of our faith is God. Armstrong may have identified the major cause for the anemia of the church. But what seems even clearer is the fact that the most neglected part of the clergy's vocation is theology. Being competent theologians is the crying need of the professional ministry today. The laity of the church need, and are seeking, ministerial leadership that helps them discern and understand the will of God for their lives. The clergy must have enough theological perception to enable church members to make sense of their lives and the faith they are trying to live. Periods of renewal have always been led by the church's pastor-theologians. Today's clergy need to be clearheaded as well as kindhearted. While caring, counseling, and organizing have their roles to play in contemporary ministry, the journey out of cultural bondage will be led by those who not only outlive but outthink the cultural pharoahs who wield secular power.

Much is being said today about clergy stress and clergy burnout, two problems once thought to be confined to secular employment. The Alban Institute has produced manuals to help clergy cope with these problems.[18] Yet it is interesting that the manuals do not consider the possibility that clergy stress may be directly related to ministerial enculturation. While most clergy are well intentioned and sincere people, the truth is that we are as enculturated as our church members are. Financial security, power, prestige, degrees, and other types of cultural success standards have become primary concerns for the clergy. The cultural ladder of success, which those under stress in secular occupations have tried to climb, tempts the clergy as well.

The minister who is a theologian, however, knows faithfulness is the measure of success in ministry. The fact that the desire for cultural success has become so prominent among clergy lies in our failure to be firmly rooted in theology. To a significant degree, clergy have lost their focus on the biblical underpinnings of church and ministry.

All this suggests that clergy stress and burnout have enculturated roots. It may be that today's ministerial leadership has allowed ministry to become a profession rather than a vocation. As a consequence, both laity and clergy alike have become enculturated. Many of the problems besetting the church may be at the doorstep of its leadership more than anywhere else.

This being the case, disciplined study cannot be viewed as an option in ministry. Clergy who claim not to have enough time for serious study do not understand the nature of ministry or recognize the threat enculturation poses. When other roles crowd out study, the minister is simply too busy with other roles. Management of time is not a new problem in the ministry, but for us to allow our own needs and the expectations of others to cause us to neglect study is in itself a sign of the influence of enculturation on us. Disciplined study is often difficult and seldom gains public recognition. Yet its absence only leaves the clergy more harried and unfocused. This frustrates the laity who have no one else to turn to for theological guidance.

None of this should suggest that the clergy should sit in their studies thinking about ministry instead of doing it. For this reason the servant-leader model of ministry may be the necessary practical framework within which the clergy functions as theologians.[19] Ministers are not leaders by directing. We are leaders by serving. We must model the gospel we proclaim, as the power to do so is given to us. We should not forget that Joshua was a military general; St. Paul, a tentmaker; Karl Barth, a small town pastor; Dietrich Bonhoeffer, a political activist; and Martin Luther King, Jr., a civil rights organizer. Commitment to being a theologian who is at the same time a servant-leader is one of the ways ministry can remain a vocation rather than a profession.

Step Eight: Doing Ministry by Call
This step is closely related to the previous one and naturally

follows from it. For the minister who is a theologian knows that ministry is never simply a profession but is a holy calling, i.e., a vocation. Ministry is done by those who sense that God has called them into service, a call that has been confirmed within the community of faith. It is certainly true that a call is often very difficult to discern. The story of the call of Samuel (*1 Samuel 3:1-18*) describes the difficulty of recognizing the difference between the voice of God and human voices. But this cannot and should not become an excuse for ignoring the dimension of call in ministry.

Denominational life in America is very close to enculturating call to the point where it has become meaningless. Often call is little more than the next step up the professional ladder and/or a move to a higher paying position. At the root of the problem is our failure to continue to undergird ministry with theology. When we lose our theological bearings, we have nothing to fall back on except the concepts that our culture offers.

It may be that denominations as a whole will have to change the process of ministerial placement in order for call to have a place in it. Perhaps salary should be discussed only after call has been confirmed by the minister and the congregation or agency. In this way, our will to serve by call might undergo an important testing. At the very least, every minister who seeks to serve Christ's church should attempt to apply call in practical ways. Those who do not struggle with the issue of call have no hope that ministry can have integrity.

The issue of call also applies to congregations. In seeking ordained ministerial leadership, members of a congregation need to commit themselves to applying call to the process. The minister they do call should be the one who, they are convinced, is the person God is sending them. This means search committees, and the congregation as a whole, should spend time in prayer, seeking clarity of God's will for the life of that congregation.

Our way of thinking about call can and must be changed. There is every assurance from the Bible that those who ask will receive, those who seek will find, and those who knock will have the door opened to them (*Matthew 7:7*). As we have noted, discernment of call is extremely difficult. After all, we walk by faith rather than sight (*2 Corinthians 5:7*). But without the desire to know genuine call, ministry is lost to enculturation completely.

In the end, doing ministry by call is a challenge to the depth and quality of the prayer life of church members and clergy. For without prayer there is little chance that we will recognize God's call in the ways he makes it known to us today.

Step Nine: De-Americanizing the Gospel

This step seems to suggest a type of deprogramming of people who have experienced some type of brainwashing. We do not have anything quite so radical in mind. Yet it is important to underscore the fact that Americanization of the gospel is both a serious and pervasive problem in the American church. Generations of Christians in this country have grown up taking for granted the notion that God has especially blessed America above other nations. An American civil religion[20] has become a part of the church's self-understanding, so that it is difficult for church members to recognize the difference between civil religion and Christianity.

One of the primary ways for the church to de-Americanize the gospel is through the promotion of the concept of world citizenship. We can teach the concept of the sovereignty of God to emphasize that he is Creator of the world, making all peoples God's people. Children and adults can be taught about the church in other lands, learning about the cultures of those nations in the process. Perhaps we can even learn something of the way Christians in other lands view Christians in America.

One of the things some denominations are doing is linking a congregation here in America with one in another nation. Communications and even exchange visits among the ministers and laity are arranged. In some areas, groups of Christians have traveled to another nation, with a group from that country visiting these Christians in America.

There are many ways we can build the concept of global citizenship. Each time we do, we remind ourselves that the God who blesses America also blesses other nations. This is the God whose son came to save not only Americans but also the whole world.

Yet we must be candid in admitting that the task of building a sense of global citizenship in America is a formidable one. Factors such as geographical and psychological isolationism make the challenge difficult. But even more problematic is the deep-rooted belief we Americans have that the rest of the world should be American. We really do believe that America, as Lincoln once described it, is "the last best hope for mankind." We are not content to be a great nation. Our political leaders seem to feel the necessity to use superlatives when speaking of our country. We are not a great nation, but the *greatest* nation on earth. We are not a leader among nations, but *the* leader, and seem to be determined to remain in front. It is as if our identity would be destroyed if we were forced to think of ourselves as simply one among other great nations. This is in part why the new world we live in, where we are *not* number one in everything from building cars to military power, is causing much uneasiness about our place in world affairs.

The church must be "tough-minded" about the forces that work against the growth of the concept of global citizenship here in America. In some instances, Christians who promote the concept may be viewed with suspicion and may even be criticized for being unpatriotic. Should this happen, we must stand firm in the conviction that promoting global citizenship is a practical way of remaining both Christian and American, in that order. To do less is to compromise the integrity of our commitment to be a covenant people.

The church, of course, cannot simply talk about global citizenship, it must also practice it. This will require Christians in American churches to teach and preach a gospel that is radically uncompromising in its reverence for the universal sovereignty of God. We need to be keenly aware of the danger of attitudes and views which promote nationalism above the universality of God's saving act of grace in Jesus Christ. At the same time, Christians in America must be responsible in both faith and patriotism so as not to attempt to "baptize" the American Constitution. We should lead the way in protecting the freedom of choice for all citizens, which may include the choice not to be Christian or religious at all.

The Christian community does not benefit from religious nationalism. It loses more than it ever gains when patriotism and faith in God become indistinguishable. The Christian church's message knows no geographical or political boundaries. De-Americanization of the gospel is possible only if this fact remains clear in the minds of American Christians. It will remain clear if we read and study the biblical tradition with honesty and candor as well as faith. The Bible leaves no doubt that the dividing line between the true and the false prophet was the former's commitment to the universal sovereignty of God and the latter's rejection of it.[21]

Thus, any congregation which seeks to maintain the integrity of the Christian gospel by de-Americanizing it stands in that "true prophet" tradition. Moreover, in doing so it serves well both God and country.

Summary

Practical steps need to be taken as the church attempts to break loose from cultural bondage in order to renew its covenant as the people of God. These steps will help clarify for the church its own call to ministry and, at the same time, will help to reestablish the integrity of the church's witness in the world. Spirit and structure go together. How we do things is as important as what we think. Changes that can effectively stem the tide of enculturation need to be implemented by the church now. This is not a time for waiting. The capacity for making these changes to a certain extent depends upon our relationship with Christ, but making them can also have the effect of deepening this relationship. We need to step into the water.

This is also a time to teach in the church. Teaching nurtures experiential faith and guides the practical ways we live out our faith. We now turn our thoughts to the role of education in covenant renewal.

3

Covenant Teaching

Education is the means by which a group passes its traditions from one generation to another, whether this is done in formal or informal ways. This is, of course, true for the church. But education in the faith community is of a special kind. It must take its lead from the nature of the gospel that is taught. This means the subject shapes the way it is taught in the church.

Because of enculturation, this principle of education in the church has been significantly compromised. The way Christian education is done in the church is itself an extension and perpetuation of enculturation. Beyond the structural problems of limited instructional time, education in the church has tamed the radicalness of the gospel. Rather than classes creating a learning experience, in most cases they create an environment of belonging. That is, *social relations* are the center of activity in church education rather than learning.

In one respect this situation has a positive influence. In the midst of modern fragmentation, it is appropriate for the church to provide a sense of belonging for people. We all need to find groups where our names are remembered and our presence is considered important. We need to experience being cared about, as well as having the opportunity to be caregivers ourselves.

Socialization through church school classes can also nurture loyalty to the church. Class membership can become the point of entry into the life of the church as a whole. Class identity can lead to church identification. Loyalty to a particular class can be the seedbed of loyalty to the church.

But as commendable as church loyalty can be, and important as a sense of belonging is to us, neither of these necessarily translates into commitment to Christ when we are confronted with moral/ethical decisions or with temptations to idolatry. In its most negative impact, enculturation leads church members to substitute belonging to a class for belonging to Christ, to substitute loyalty to a church for loyalty to Christ. It is a paradox that church school members, sometimes more than any other group, resist the gospel's radicalness when it is taught. It is as if the gospel is unwelcome in the educational ministry of the church because of fear that it will disrupt the social cohesion within classes.

Significant changes are needed in the way Christian education is organized on the congregational level, demanding the best thinking we possess. Education in the church plays a significant role in contributing to or limiting the influence of enculturation. The choice is ours to make. Choosing the latter, though, means reacquainting ourselves with the true nature of the biblical gospel. That nature can be characterized in three ways.

Teaching the True Source of Life

The first characteristic of the gospel is that it points to a source of life beyond culture. Moreover, this source of life is what Christian education points us to; it is both subject and object in learning for the Christian. The writer of John's Gospel makes this point about the gospel when he so eloquently wrote:

Now Jesus did many other signs in the presence of the disciples, which are not written in this book; but these are written that you may believe that Jesus is the Christ, the Son of God, and that believing you may have life in his name (*20:30-31*).

The writer was addressing people who were already Christians. They had experienced the reality of the raised Christ. His purpose in writing was to strengthen them in that experience. Believing Jesus is the Christ[22] involves intellectual understanding, but the Gospel writer wants his readers to go beyond the intellectual level to the experiential level. He wants them to have "life" in Jesus' name (*v. 31*), "life" which contradicts cultural notions about life and where life is found.

Life in the name of Jesus Christ is the goal of the church's educational ministry, giving our teaching its peculiar thrust. Knowledge plays an important role in achieving this goal. In Christian education, knowledge is always a means to a greater end, never an end in itself. In the church's teaching ministry, knowledge, in a sense, is an offering we make to God. We place what we know at the altar and ask God to use it to deepen our experience of his presence through our knowledge. We cannot create such an experience. Rather, we offer our knowledge to God and pray for his spirit to turn it into experience (see *John 14:25-26*).

Enculturation has blurred this goal of Christian education, leading us to some serious problems. One is an anti-intellectualism which views scholarship as an enemy of faith. Those Christians who have this attitude see the role of teaching as apologetic—that is, as a defense of true faith. They reject modern biblical scholarship as liberalism which undermines the authority of the Bible.

Anti-intellectualism requires a dogmatic approach to teaching in the church. Metaphors in the Bible are elevated to the level of doctrines which, in turn, must be accepted on face value. Moreover, inerrancy of scripture becomes a necessity in anti-intellectualism. The authority of the Bible is externalized, making it essential that it is taught as inerrant and infallible. The authority of inerrant scripture then becomes the authority of the teacher. Church members are told, "The Bible says . . . ," and thus what the teacher says is to be accepted because he/she is supposedly teaching what the Bible says, which is not to be questioned because it is inerrant.

This kind of anti-intellectualism puts the gospel on an emotional level. It attempts to coerce the believer into blind acceptance of doctrines and ideas which may not even square with human experience in general and/or which may actually contradict the life and teachings of Jesus. Therefore, it contributes little that is positive in nurturing faith. Ironically, in this way it makes it easier for enculteration's influence in the church to grow.

A second problem enculturation has created in our teaching ministry is just the opposite of the first. It is a predominately *intellectual approach* to teaching. This attitude places emphasis on the acquisition of knowledge as an end in itself. It seeks to objectify study in the name of intellectual objectivity. In this approach scholarship is a tool for understanding but not for strengthening faith. The latter is viewed as inappropriate for objective study which seeks to maintain intellectual integrity from a purely scientific point of view.

Each of these problems feeds on the other. Anti-intellectualism invites objectivism, and vice versa, while the gospel being caught in the middle. Neither strengthens the kind of faith experience scripture describes as possible for us. In their own way these approaches obscure truth, rather than reveal it, because at best they teach half-truths.

As might be expected, teaching in the church that takes experiential faith seriously lies somewhere between these two extremes. It is a two-fold approach. On the one hand, it seeks to help Christians hear the theological message of scripture. Its focus is neither doctrinal nor historical. Rather, it is one of attempting to *listen* to the biblical text to hear what the word of the Lord is for today's church.[23] From this perspective scholarship is seen as essential to an informed faith, yet scholarship does not become an end in itself. Instead, it serves to help contemporary Christians truly hear what the text is saying to them. It seeks to enable the one listening to move from what the text meant to what it means.

One of the ways listening to the text is achieved is to hear the biblical message as story.[24] It is the story of God's gracious acts of redemption in Israel and in Jesus Christ. It is the story of the faith and disobedience of our ancestors in the faith. The story is never abstract. Rather, it is always specific. It describes the struggle of God with particular people, families, and nations as he attempted to work his will for all creation in and through them. The story is often very simple, told without concern for contradiction or conflict. It says what it says, inviting the listener to make connections between what God has done and what he is still doing. Further, the story asks for a response. In its telling there is the challenge to act upon what is heard. It leaves no room for one to be a bystander. We either accept the challenge God's story puts before us, or we walk away (*Mark 10:22*).

Listening to the story of the Bible allows us to confront the text as it now stands. How it reached its present form is less important than what it now says in its canonical form. Further, listening to the text presumes we do not listen alone. God is the giver of life (*Genesis 1:1*) and the giver of faith (*1 Corinthians 12:3*). Our willingness to listen will be matched by his desire to give us both life and faith. It is in receiving each of these gifts that we gain our sense of identity as people of covenant, covenant that is not imposed but that is written on our hearts (*Jeremiah 31:33*). The story has within it the gift of life.

The second part of this approach to teaching is that it nurtures us in wisdom for living. Life style and identity are inextricably bound in experiential faith. This means moral and ethical dimensions of the gospel story ask for exploration. They cannot be imposed. Moral and ethical teachings are not written on stone. They, too, must be written on the heart of the believer.

This is what happens when we are nurtured in wisdom.[25] That nurture occurs as we learn the ways our ancestors in the faith have attempted to live as people of covenant in their own time in history. Teaching that nurtures us in wisdom seeks to explore all the Bible has to say about a moral/ethical issue confronting us.[26] That search must be honest and candid enough to admit at times that the biblical tradition has little or nothing to say about an issue. It must also be willing to admit the multiplicity of views on the same issue that may be found in the Bible.

Then the task of the teaching of wisdom is to discern any consistent pattern that emerges when the views in the Bible on the issue being studied are carefully examined. It is in this emergence of a pattern that we are most helped in learning how to respond today to the moral/ethical questions confronting us.

The teaching of wisdom is not a simple task. It is rooted in the paradox of faith that God has revealed his will in scripture, and yet we are not always able to discern it.[27] It suggests that we have to be cautious in speaking of the will of God in specific terms, while at the same time we must attempt always to be specific and must guard against making careless generalizations. But we can be sure that we are becoming "wiser" when we are able to affirm that there are always shades of grey in making moral/ethical decisions, yet we are willing to make them nonetheless. At the very least we know that God wills both wholeness and community for his world and our lives. Whatever decisions we make must contribute something to one or both of these (wholeness and community).

Teaching wisdom dares to trust that the Holy Spirit will write the law upon our hearts. It tests the conviction undergirding our discussion that we can know Christ's presence and be strengthened by him to live faithfully. Teaching wisdom admits to the weaknesses of human flesh while confessing faith in the power of the gospel story to save.

Subversive Teaching

A second characteristic of the gospel we teach is its *subversiveness*. The nature of the gospel is subversive; therefore, Christian education is by nature subversive. But we must define carefully what this means in the life of the church.

To subvert literally means to turn from beneath; to overturn, or overthrow from the foundation. This is precisely what the gospel is supposed to do. It is to overturn and overthrow the very foundations of the world. It is to turn things upside down and inside out, to make the last first and the first last. This is because we worship a God who makes the earth reel and rock, the foundations of the earth tremble (*Psalm 18:7; Isaiah 24:18*). The God of our faith is the One who speaks and every valley is lifted up, every mountain and hill made low, the uneven ground is made level, and the rough places become as a plain (*Isaiah 40:3-4*).

But enculturation has led us to try to "tame" God, to domesticate him, if you will, as if he were the supporter of the order we create. This has meant that to a significant degree we have been teaching a gospel that accommodates itself to cultural values, a gospel that lives in peaceful coexistence with society. But such accommodation ignores the fact that the values in the kingdom of Heaven are in conflict with the values in the kingdoms of the earth. Creation is in a state of rebellion against God. The church is called to be the alternative community which stands over against the world, seeking to end the rebellion and to break the stubborn will of those who refuse to acknowledge God as God.

One of our problems in the church is that we have not realized how subversive love is. Overturning anything is perceived as requiring violence. But that is to fail to understand the power of love to turn things upside down. Love subverts stubborn rebellion. It possesses the power to overturn the existing order, the status quo. The resistance to Jesus by those who did not understand him testifies to the power of love to upset the existing social order.

The modern church has lost its cutting edge as a result of privatizing and spiritualizing the gospel. We have accustomed ourselves to the status quo. What is worse, as Christian Americans we have deluded ourselves into believing ours is a Christian nation. We have failed to see or have been unwilling to see that capitalism is not the economics of justice but the economics of profit, which means that greed and the struggle for power dominate.

The weakness in the church's teaching ministry lies in the fact that it has not emphasized the mission Christ has given us as his church to penetrate culture in order to bring a reordering of its loyalties and values. Going into the world to teach the gospel, especially as we live it, inevitably involves conflict with the existing order. Furthermore, when someone becomes a disciple, the status quo has not only lost another friend but also gained a foe.

In *Acts* there is an incident where this is exactly what happened. It is the story of a woman's conversion at Philippi (*16:10-40*). Paul and Silas, following Paul's vision of God calling them to preach in Macedonia, travelled to Philippi. One of their converts was a slave girl who was believed to have the power of "divination" (*v. 16*), the power to tell the future of a person who approached her. Her owners used her to make money as their seer. In the encounter Paul called out the spirit of divination, leaving her without the power her owners had used to make money.

The owners angrily seized Paul and Silas, taking them to the authorities with the charge, "These men are Jews and they are disturbing our city. They advocate customs which it is not lawful for us Romans to accept or practice" (*vs. 20- 21*).[28] The crowds supported the owners. The authorities ordered Paul and Silas stripped, beaten, and thrown into prison.

The irony of the story is that the owners told the truth. Paul and Silas were disturbing the city. The gospel always does. This incident should remind us of the gospel's power to disturb. To teach in word and deed the kingdom of God requires of us a keen perception of what is in our hands. We are wielding the "hammer of the Lord" (*Jeremiah 23:29*) that breaks down injustice and threatens the oppresser. The gospel's power to save and transform cannot work without disturbing the status quo. Therefore, the church cannot be naive about the conflict that is inevitable when its message and mission collide with modern power brokers who have vested interests in the way things are. The church is out to subvert their power. They know this; so must we.

This means that in our teaching we must not only know our own story as God's people. At the same time we must be educated about the realities of the surrounding culture. Education in the church must not be party to the perpetuation of cultural myths that would have us believe America is a Christian nation or that Americans are God's specially chosen people to lead the world in righteousness. Acknowledging what is good about American society does not require us to become deaf, dumb, and blind to what is not good.

In a real sense the subversive nature of the gospel puts the challenge before the church's teaching ministry to decide whether or not we will "obey God rather than men" (*Acts 5:29*). Yet the decision is not only a choice between loyalties. It is also a matter of inner security. The choice to obey God cannot be made if the church is dependent upon the world for its support and honor. As with individuals, a congregation whose inward life is not rooted in the security which comes from trust in God will not have the strength to be subversive. As a result, that congregation's teaching ministry will offer no enlightenment, encouragement, and strategy to its members regarding the conflict between Christ and culture. But the congregation whose inward life is deeply rooted in the desire to be faithful, rather than successful, will equip its members to be ambassadors for Christ, God making his appeal through them (*2 Corinthians 5:20*).

Teaching Community

The third factor that reveals the radicalness of the gospel is the emphasis on community. In the church's teaching ministry, the difference between the gospel being personal but not private must be made clear. Yet our teaching is often guilty of privatizing the gospel. Scriptural applications and illustrations tend to be exclusively individualistic. Scripture lessons have the individual class member, rather than the church as a whole, as their focus.

Teaching in the church needs to have as its goal the creating of a vision for a new *community* of people who are devoted to God and are doing his will. Personal moral/ethical application of the gospel is certainly a part of this vision. But the final goal of our teaching is the building of church, and that is always communal, never individualistic. The challenge responsible teaching puts to us is not simply what kind of person we are but what kind of church we belong to.

This goal seems an obvious one, yet it is often neglected. A visit to most Sunday school classes in any church will reveal teaching that nurtures and perpetuates privatization of the gospel. Classes focus on meeting the needs of individual members. There is almost a complete lack of awareness of how classes can contribute to the corporate identity and mission of the church. There is little sense of the role individual parts (classes) play in the body as a whole. Therefore, a sense of responsibility for the quality of the corporate life of a congregation is missing almost entirely.

It is here that Christians have much to learn from our Jewish brothers and sisters. The personal identity of an individual Jew is inextricably bound up with being a member of the Jewish community. There is no separation between the individual and the community. The power of individual Jews exists for the sake of the community as a whole. They know that God calls a people who have a corporate identity and a corporate mission.

The communal nature of the gospel is directly related to its subversive dimension. The church as the body of Christ stands over and against culture. The strength of individuals to resist the influences of accommodation is derived from the community. We often say that a chain is no stronger than its weakest link. But this is not the case with the church. The church consists entirely of weak links which, in the linking together, God makes stronger than any individual members. The key lies in being bound together.

It is important, however, for us to realize that we must be careful to define community in its most universal sense. The communal nature of the gospel has an ecumenical character in today's church. It simply is not enough for individual congregations or denominations to nurture corporate identity that leads to sectarianism. Unless we are able to identify ourselves as the church universal, we miss the sense of community to which Christ calls us. The oneness we are called to manifest (*John 17*) is universal, not denominational.

What is at stake in the universal nature of community is the presence of Christ in the church. Father Raymond Brown has shown us that what was "new" about the new commandment Jesus gave to his disciples to love one another (*John 13:34-35*) was the fact that loving one another was one of the ways his presence would be kept among them.[29] This means that Christ's presence is linked to oneness—to community—which is the natural by-product of loving one another. The extent to which we love one another determines the quality of community and the degree to which we experience the presence of Christ among us.

But the universal nature of community has yet another dimension. *John 13:35* suggests that the quality of community will determine the effectiveness of our witness as Christ's church. Others will know we are his disciples by our love for one another.[30] In other words, the church's mission of witness cannot be separated from its communal nature. Conflict is not the only thing that divides the church and weakens its witness. Privatization of the gospel also divides the church because it separates that which by its very nature belongs together.

The church's teaching ministry can strengthen our experience of the presence of Christ and our witness in the world by placing the call to community at the center of its message. We must not apply the gospel to individuals while neglecting the call to live by the will of God as congregations. Enculturation had led us to ignore the corporate challenge of the gospel to the church itself. How we live as a church is not simply an extension of how we live as individuals. Christian education is one of the ways we can consciously ask critical questions about the way we are living as congregations and about the extent to which enculturation has caused us to privatize the gospel.

58

Structuring Education

At this point a few rather specific suggestions about the way congregations can organize their teaching ministry may be helpful. Structure does affect spirit. *How* we do ministry has a significant impact upon *what* we do. The nature of the gospel must give shape to the church's teaching ministry. If we are serious about this, then we must also be serious about how we organize our teaching ministry. The following suggestions attempt to incorporate the three characteristics of the gospel previously discussed.

Class Covenant

Socialization has become an important element in the church school classes. The need and desire to belong makes us resistant to changes that may alter the established identity and relationships that classes have created. This may be the single most influential factor in our willingness to continue doing education in the church in a way that is dominated by enculturation.

The good news, however, is that socialization can be achieved in many ways other than the way we now organize church school classes. The fact that the gospel creates a community can be the basis for creating classes that provide us with a feeling of belonging. Belonging which is a by-product of genuine Christian community expands the possibilities for us to experience it beyond a single class membership. Belonging can develop in any group when Christian community is the power that binds us together.

A practical way of making community tangible is the use of a class covenant. This covenant is a written statement that expresses what it means to belong to Christ and to one another in an educational setting. Below is an example of such a covenant.

* * * * * * * * * *

Covenant describes a relationship in which those involved give and receive from one another. If mutual enrichment is possible, however, there must also be an acceptance of responsibilities for the life shared together.

This class is an extension of the covenantal life we have as

Christ's church. If this class is to help us mature in our faith, each member must be willing to accept specific responsibilities for our life together. These responsibilities include:

1. regular and punctual attendance at each class session
2. faithful preparation of class assignments
3. daily prayer for each class member
4. willingness to listen to new ideas and be stretched in uncomfortable ways
5. commitment to inform the class (or teacher) if the class cannot be completed

Acceptance of these responsibilities expresses our willingness to contribute to one another's growth and development as people of covenant. We, therefore, enter into this relationship with joy and in the expectation that this study will deepen our faith and broaden our understanding of what it means to be Christ's church.

Several important elements of this covenant merit highlighting. First, the covenant ties the church's educational ministry to the biblical tradition of promise and covenant. This creates the proper environment for learning to occur, affirming the church's story which provides its identity and defines its mission.

Second, the disciplines of the covenant invite class members to take ultimate responsibility for their life together. Becoming a class member means one is committed to praying for the class and its members daily. Every covenant member knows that he/she is being held up in prayer by all the other members. It also means that everyone is praying for the Holy Spirit to use the class to make the presence of Christ known to each person. In addition, daily prayers will include petitions for the Spirit to use the class to strengthen the life of the entire congregation.

A third advantage is that the class covenant makes clear that education in the church involves commitment. The covenant does not permit spectator membership. A commitment of time and study is expected from every member. The covenant is a tangible way to bind class members to one another. It leaves no doubt that the life of one member enriches all the others when membership is taken seriously, and it diminishes all the others when it is not. In short, the covenant asks each person to make learning a priority.

Finally, the covenant has intrinsic power to strengthen all the members to keep it. There is strength in shared commitment that is absent when individuals move in and out of a class at will. Making a commitment to others binds us together in a way that *draws out the best* that is in us. This is a very important factor in the use of a covenant that cannot be overemphasized.

Implicit in the covenant is the fact that the class has a definite beginning and ending. This is also an essential element in using a covenant. Learning in the church, like discipleship, should be a conscious choice rather than an assumption. When we decide to enter into covenant with others, we are choosing to learn. The importance of this choice should be obvious. Learning has to be something we choose to do if real learning is to occur. Being a class member in itself does not mean one has a desire to learn. But when one chooses to enter into covenant with others, there is good reason to believe a desire to learn is present, though others factors may also influence a person to join.

One of the problems with existing church school classes is that they have no end. They seem to go on forever. It is easy for the original purpose of the class, learning, to become secondary to the existence of the class. Moreover, there is no flexibility for one to move to a different class without dropping out of the present one, which creates further problems. It is amazing that people who were educated in schools where classes changed constantly allow (or want) the church to have no such flexibility or diversification. Joining a Sunday school class is a "life sentence" in most churches. Once one is in, there is no constructive way of getting out.

A class covenant works no magic, but it does offer a tangible way for congregations to allow the nature of the gospel itself to influence what we teach and how we teach it.

The Issue of Time

A word needs to be addressed to the issue of time regarding the church's teaching ministry. As we have noted, actual instruction time is severely limited in the existing structure. If we are serious about learning in the church, then something has to be done about this situation. It is true that holding classes during the week is one alternative. But Sunday morning classes cannot be left in their existing condition. These are where most learning takes place, if it takes place at all. Yet no reasonable person can argue that thirty to forty minutes of instruction once a week can be called education. No parent would allow such a travesty in secular education. But these same parents allow Christian education to be done this way for their children and themselves.

A simple step in the right direction would be for the Sunday school hour to be moved up one hour ahead of its present starting time. This has the advantage of using the established Sunday school structure more effectively. It may be that, given the busy schedules families follow today, expanding the existing Sunday school program to a reasonable time for study offers the best hope of attracting them to serious Christian education.

Curriculum

Curriculum is another practical concern that cannot be ignored. We shall say very little about curriculum, however, for resources on a multitude of curriculum alternatives are readily available. What we can say is that any church school curriculum should have diversity. The notion of everyone studying the same material is an absurdity. The needs and interests of church members are themselves very diverse and should guide congregations in developing curriculum. One word of caution, however, is that in this variety we are suggesting the Bible should not be neglected. Unfortunately, in cases where attempts to diversify curriculum have been tried, this is precisely what has often happened. This is especially true among young and middle-aged adults, where self-help and pop-psychology books have been overused.

Church members today do not need less Bible study. We need more; more, that is, instead of the piecemeal approach used by the International Uniform Series. The Bible is the church's book, and should be a significant part of education in the church. The more we study the Bible, the more we realize how much more there is to learn.

Teacher Training

Finally, we must say something about teacher training. One positive sign in public education today is the renewed emphasis upon the quality of teaching. Pressure is growing for teachers at all levels to be competent as a result of extensive and intensive training in their fields. Here is one instance where the church can learn something positive from secular education.

The contemporary church should have no hesitancy in holding to the same standards regarding its teachers. Teachers in the church bear an awesome responsibility for passing on the traditions of our faith. The task cannot be done in a responsible way unless they have had, and continue to have, extensive teaching training. Sincerity and a willing spirit are important, but in themselves they do not equip a person to teach in the church. Teacher training is simply indispensible in the life of the church.

What is more, the rising educational level of children today makes teacher preparation in the church all the more urgent. Christian education will maintain credibility only as long as those who teach it have credibility. Church school teachers cannot, for example, present the gospel as if there is a three- storey universe (hell, earth, heaven) to students who study about galaxies and black holes. Teachers in the church need to learn how to teach the gospel story without expecting students to give up all sense of reality. They must understand that the Bible speaks the truth of God in the idiom of its own world and that this truth does not require us to ignore all the knowledge about God's world that has been learned since the Bible was written.

Teachers in the church need theological education. The church has always expected its ordained leadership to be theologically educated. Yet we have supposed that those who teach the message preached by the ordained do not need such education, which may say a great deal about the church's view of the importance of education. But this situation must be changed. Efforts have been made to offer church school teachers training. At best, however, these have been limited in scope and opportunity.

The one person who holds the key to teacher preparation is the ordained minister. The one who has had the benefit of theological education has the responsibility for training the laity to teach. Required classes for teachers need to be a systematic part of the educational ministry of the church. Anyone who is unwilling to attend these classes should not teach others. In most instances, church school teachers will welcome the help. Many of them feel woefully lacking in their task. Through neglect, the clergy have nurtured the notion that serious theological training is unnecessary for those who teach in the church.

A well trained core of teachers who feel a sense of call to the church's teaching ministry can have a significant impact on the total life of the church. Indeed, teacher training is one of the primary ways the church can turn the tide against enculturation.

Summary

The nature of the gospel must shape the church's vital ministry of education. The church's teaching must reflect the experiential, subversive, and communal qualities of our faith. The task of education is to create an alternative community that stands over against cultural values and idolatries. As we allow the gospel to shape our teaching, particular practical changes in the way we organize the church's educational ministry will also have to be made. Structure and spirit should not be separated.[31]

4

Covenant Preaching

Several years ago, the German pastor and theologian Helmut Thielicke wrote a book about preaching. The American translation had the intriguing title, *The Trouble with the Church.*[32] It was an appropriate title. Thielicke argues that there was an essential relationship between preaching and the quality of the church's life.

Thielicke's thesis is an important insight that should not be lost. Preaching is not simply one element in the church's total ministry. It is the cornerstone of ministry. The proclamation of the word affects every other part of church life as nothing else does. Everything that has been discussed up to this point needs to find its way into the church's preaching ministry. And we should understand that preaching belongs to the church, not simply the clergy. The church's prophetic, pastoral, and visionary roles should be energized by preaching. This is why a chapter on preaching concerns the laity as well as the clergy.

But even more, the laity need to understand what preaching is. The pulpit has no place or power apart from the pew. Energizing the church's preaching ministry will require more than the clergy's efforts. The laity have to participate in great preaching. They do so primarily by approaching the preaching event expectant of hearing some word of the Lord for their lives. The attitude of the laity has a significant impact upon the quality of preaching. This is not to suggest that a congregation can make poor sermons into good ones. But a congregation that expects nothing from a sermon will usually get it.

The laity (and even clergy) need to learn what makes preaching-preaching. Too often good preaching, from the perspective of the laity, has more to do with delivery than content. In addition, what is thought to be good preaching is sometimes little more than hearing what one wants to hear rather than what needs to be heard. But neither delivery nor pablum preaching can enliven the church. The only kind of preaching that can do that is preaching that brings together the word from scripture and the lives of the congregational members, wherein the presence of God is experienced. This may not happen all the time or at the same time to all those who are gathered. But it can and does happen. Preaching, therefore, has a central role to play in covenant renewal. This is why clergy and laity alike need to gain a fresh perspective and new appreciation of what it means for the word to be proclaimed in the life of a congregation.

This chapter has been written to educate the laity to what preaching is. Yet it will no doubt read as if it is directed to the clergy. It is difficult to write about preaching without writing to the clergy. Perhaps in this regard the lay readers will be eavesdropping on this chapter. If so, I can only hope you will be close enough to hear what is actually being said. Without a resurgence of preaching the church's life will remain anemic. Such a resurgence will require the joint efforts of both the clergy and laity.

The modern church has lived through a period of time when preaching was thought to be dead. We are now far enough removed from these voices of doom to know that announcements of the demise of preaching were premature. Yet we have to confess there is much that is wrong with the pulpit today. While preaching is not dead, there continues to be a lot of dead preaching. Moreover the pulpit has become a rather weak voice in challenging the church's enculturation. Indeed, enculturation itself seems to have a significant influence on today's preaching for several reasons.

One is that preaching often lacks a biblical basis, and thus fails to evoke our memory of whose we are as the church. That is, much of the preaching today fails to tell the story of God's gracious acts and the call to obedience he has set before us. What this translates into is a serious lack of biblically based preaching. By this we mean preaching that has done its exegetical homework. Too many sermons reflect neglect in the hard work of struggling with a biblical text in a serious way. Topical preaching, in which biblical texts are only alluded to, seems to dominate the pulpit. Often, texts are used merely to support a sermon rather than the sermon flowing from the text. The best of topical preaching leaves no doubt that the preacher has seriously engaged the biblical text. Unfortunately much topical preaching today is not the best.

A second cause for the pulpit's failure to challenge enculturation is that it comes up short in nurturing church members in moral/ethical discernment. In part this is because there is an appalling neglect in addressing the critical moral/ethical issues facing our world. In times of national crisis or internal struggles for justice, many pulpits are silent. There was a period during the civil rights movement of the '60s when the clergy attempted to address this issue from the pulpit, sometimes facing severe criticism from church members for doing so. That experience of challenging the church's cultural bondage regarding racial bigotry seems, however, to have left us more timid than ever to face up to social issues from the pulpit.

Today the nuclear arms race is challenging the church's powers of moral/ethical discernment. Yet the voices from American pulpits are amazingly quiet on this issue. A few notable exceptions can be cited. But the fact is that they *are* exceptions. That is the problem. Church members are inundated with a wide range of political views on the arms race issue. But they also need to hear some word from the pulpit that seeks to intersect the biblical tradition with this vital issue. This in fact needs to be the strongest voice they hear. Being church members means they are Christians *first,* and their attitude toward the arms race (or any other social issue) should reflect their discipleship.

This is not to suggest the pulpit should provide *the* answer to moral dilemmas. But it should and must raise questions that need to be discussed in the church regarding moral/ethical issues. One of the problems, of course, is that some preaching, especially on the airways, does attempt to give the only answer to moral questions. Some television preachers speak as if they have received the final word of the Lord on every subject. They seem to assume that their interpretation of the Bible and God's will are one and the same.

This is not the kind of preaching we are advocating. Moral pronouncements are not preaching. But preaching includes, in fact is, preaching one's convictions. There is a thin line between the two, warranting caution when sermons confront moral issues. That preaching has to address these issues, however, there should be no question.

A third factor that weakens preaching is the clergy's failure to see the power of preaching. The fact that sermon preparation often becomes the last item on the minister's weekly schedule indicates that the clergy do not understand the power preaching has in shaping a congregation's life. It is inconceivable that ministers would neglect sermon preparation were they aware of the crucial role preaching can play.

Most ministers enjoy preaching. But the present state of preaching suggests that most do not make weekly sermon preparation a high priority. Ministers are faced with far more demands than hours in a day. This means preparation time for sermons has to be a disciplined commitment. Perhaps the problem lies in the fact that ministers are poor managers of their time. But the real problem seems to be that ministers have lost confidence in the power of preaching, and question whether the spoken word has any lasting impact.

From a purely human point of view, political elections should awaken us to the power of oratory. Politicians who are skilled speakers usually become successful politicians. President Reagan is an excellent example of the power that is in the hands of someone skilled in communications. Few people give him high marks for his grasp of issues or his ability to state facts accurately. Yet he continues to win public support for his policies primarily because of the persuasive power of his spoken word.

The minister, however, does not seek simply to be successful. Preaching is more than political rhetoric. Preaching is an act of God. His Spirit gives the power of utterance. His word is the truth that is spoken. His message becomes a fire in people's souls. Those who step into a pulpit speak more than a human word. They possess the words of eternal life (*John 6:68*).

This is why preaching has power, a power that is born out of the power of scripture itself. The same God who inspired the words of the Bible inspires the words of the preacher to become the vehicle for his truth to set people free.

The apostle Paul recognized the power of preaching. In *Romans 10:14-15, 17,* he wrote:

But how are men to call upon him in whom they have not believed? And how are they to believe in him of whom they have never heard? And how are they to hear without a preacher? And how can men preach unless they are sent? . . . So faith comes from what is heard, and what is heard comes by the preaching of Christ.

Here Paul makes the claim that preaching is a calling. Those who preach are sent by God to do so. Preaching is not something one decides to do. Rather, it is done only because one has been called to preach. For this reason Paul sees the emergence of faith and preaching as intimately related. Faith comes by the hearing of the word, and hearing requires the preaching of Christ. In other words, preaching makes possible the experience of the presence of Christ. The word is not simply heard but believed, i.e., experienced as true. Thus, preaching has the power to change lives!

Because preaching has this power, it is an awesome responsibility. Those who realize the power of preaching never take the task lightly nor enter into the pulpit unprepared for the event. They know that what takes place in preaching is an act of God. His creative word is let loose again and again, each time bearing the potential to create anew order out of chaos and bring light into darkness.

Scriptural Authority and Preaching

It may be that a renewal of confidence in preaching will occur only if scriptural authority can be seen from a different perspective. Modern biblical scholarship has had a profound influence upon the authority of preaching. The once sure source of authority for preaching, the Bible, is no longer so sure. Mainline Protestantism, especially the clergy, no longer accepts the inerrancy of the Bible without question. In fact, many reject it outright. The bold statement, "The Bible says . . ." now has the added phrase, "so far as I understand it." And for good reason. What anyone says the Bible says is an interpretation. Only the preacher who does not want to be honest with his congregation can deny this fact. Each of us has our particular "interpretive context," which means who we are and what we believe influence the way we understand the Bible.[33]

But this advance in biblical scholarship has created an authority crisis in the pulpit. The modern preacher speaks as "one without authority."[34] To preach from the Bible means to preach an interpretation, the effect of which has led the clergy to search for other sources of authority. Thus, we quote experts in other fields for support of our sermon thesis. While this type of supportive evidence may be helpful, our abandonment of biblical authority may have been very premature. The Bible may in fact still possess the same authority it has always had, but we have not realized it. To understand what this means, however, we must review the nature of scriptural inspiration. The inspiration and authority of the Bible are inseparable.

The recently published *Torah Commentary* of the Reform Congregations of America describes the inspiration of the Torah as follows:

> The Torah is ancient Israel's distinctive record of its search for God. It attempts to record the meeting of the human and the Divine, the great moments of encounter. Therefore, the next is often touched by the ineffable Presence. The Torah tradition testifies to a people of extraordinary spiritual sensitivity. God is not the author of the text, the people are, but God's voice may be heard through theirs if we listen with open minds.[35]

This description expresses firm belief that God has inspired the Torah's writing. His ineffable presence can be experienced by one who encounters the Torah. That encounter provides the hearer with a clear sense of identity as a member of the covenant community.

What the authors say about the Torah can be said about the Bible as a whole. The Bible is inspired because it has been touched by God's ineffable presence, providing the church with definition of identity and lifestyle. The troublesome question of inerrancy is not at issue in regard to inspiration. To put inerrancy and inspiration together externalizes inspiration (and authority), making belief in inspiration of scripture dependent upon one's acceptance of external inerrancy. The problem of linking inspiration and inerracy is made worse by the fact, as those who link the two now admit, that modern translations are not inerrant. Only the so-called "autographs" are regarded as inerrant. But all of these are now gone, and we have only imperfect copies. What then is inerrant? Something that no longer exists. To link inspiration and inerracy is, therefore, self- defeating.

If, however, inspiration means that God's presence touches the pages of the Bible and that the author's words convey his word, then clearly modern translations are as inspired as the original texts. Moreover, there are millions of Jews and Christians who are living testimony to their inspiration. Through these translations people have experienced God's presence and heard his word.

It is interesting that the Bible itself makes the claim of being inspired; specifically *2 Timothy 3:16-17:*

All scripture is inspired by God and profitable for
eaching, for reproof, for correction, and for training in
righteousness, that the man of God may be complete,
equipped for every good work.

"Inspired by God" literally means "God-breathed." Scripture, then, has been breathed by God. Another way of saying it is that the "wind of God" has moved upon scripture, suggesting what the *Torah Commentary* described as being touched by the presence of God.

This means inspiration is internal rather than external. It is not a matter of words but of God's presence. It is not something to believe in. Instead, it is something to experience. Further, in that experience we can become "complete" (*v. 17*), whole. Complete has the connotation of "put together" in the right way. Experiencing the inspiration of scripture, i.e., being touched by God's presence, can help us put our lives together in a way that gives us a sense of wholeness.

Now, if the Bible's inspiration is internal, it seems logical to conclude that its authority is also. The fact that the canon is closed and no more books will be added provides some sense of external authority to the Bible. But within the framework of what we have said about inspiration, the closing of the canon means the books in the Bible are those in which the church has experienced God's presence and heard his voice. In other words, they are not inspired because they are in the Bible. They are in the Bible because they are inspired.

This suggests that the authority of these books lies not in the fact that they are in the Bible, but, rather, in the fact that they are inspired. Further, the authority of scripture is intimately related to experiencing identity as people of covenant. When we experience God's presence and hear his voice in a biblical text, at that moment the text is both inspired and also speaks with authority. Moreover, the fact that we live in community means that this experience occurs again and again to different people with different texts, creating unity within diversity. This is why the church attributes inspiration and authority to the various books of the Bible. In its own way each offers the experience of · inspiration and authority. As Brevard Childs has put it, the Bible functions as "the vehicle for God's special communication of himself to his church and the world."[36]

Preaching has power when it trusts the internal inspiration and authority of the Bible, bringing together text and hearer so that the ineffable presence is experienced and the voice of God is heard. Then the word becomes life-giving to the community. Preaching is always an invitation to experience the word of the Lord. Its authority is experienced each time that word is experienced. If the word is not experienced, then no belief in the authority of the Bible, however strong, can give life.

From this perspective the one who preaches can do so in confidence, even as one without authority. Sermons need not appeal to an infallible source or to a notable expert. People in the pew seldom accept appeals to external authority. The authority that makes a lasting impact is one they experience within themselves. The preacher can trust the promise that God will create that experience as the biblical word is proclaimed.

Admittedly, it is difficult to conceptualize the experience in preaching of hearing the voice of God through human words. How can we put into words a feeling of being inwardly convicted by the power of a sermon? The experience no doubt has varied dimensions to it. One may be the sense of having our value system challenged. A reliable indicator of being encountered by the word of the Lord appears when the spoken word causes us to reexamine the values by which we are living. To be stirred to take the time to rethink the kind of enculturated lifestyle we may be living would suggest that God's word has been spoken to us through the human words of a sermon. Someone has said that if we read the biblical message in a way that makes us comfortable, then we can be sure that we have misread it.

Perhaps the same principle applies to preaching. The sermon that makes us feel comfortable is one in which either the word has not been preached or if preached, then not heard. There is an inescapable element of disturbance in the proclaimed word. To feel it is to know that we have heard it.

Another way of knowing the presence of God has been experienced in the preaching event, and his word heard, is when we sense a special kind of inner calm coming over us. This is not a calm that simply makes us comfortable. Rather it is the calm of inward security. When we are facing a particularly troublesome time, we may hear a sermon that gives us a feeling we can make it through the difficulties we are facing. In that moment we can trust that we have heard the word of God for us.

One other sign of having heard the word of the Lord in a sermon is when something that was said stays in our minds and will not let us go. Sometimes a persistent thought that will not leave us alone can be God's way of speaking to us. Whenever a sermon causes this to happen, we can again trust that through human words the word of God has been encountered.

Internalizing the Proclamation

The power of preaching does not lie in the one who speaks, but in the truth of the spoken message. The essence of that truth is always the presence of God. Yet the truth of the message and the messenger are inseparable. The great American preacher Phillips Brooks underscored this fact in his Lyman Beecher lectures on preaching at Yale University two centuries ago, lectures that have now become classic. Said Brooks:

There are two aspects of the minister's work, which are constantly meeting in the New Testament. They are really embodied in two words, one of which is "message" and the other is "witness". . . . In these two words together, I think, we have the fundamental conception of the matter of all Christian preaching. It is to be a message given to us for transmission, but yet a message which we cannot transmit until it has entered into our own experience, and we can give our testimony of its spiritual power.[37]

The message we preach, to have the power of credibility, is one whose truth we have experienced. This is why Brooks' own definition of "real preaching" was, "truth through personality."[38] He believed the message communicated through a person had a profound effect upon the preaching event. The messenger is not incidental to the message, but is primary to preaching.

Today's clergy must recognize that sermons which have power are those which come out of our own experience of faith, the important word being *experience*. A sermon is not an idea we want to discuss or a proposition into which we want to make inquiry. A sermon is the message God has put inside us that we have to preach. Perhaps an illustration of what we are saying will help here.

There is a minister whose weekly sermons leave no doubt about the intimate relationship he shares with his message. His congregation knows that every sermon he preaches grows out of an extensive period of getting the message inside himself before speaking it to them. The irony is that he is not a particularly dynamic public speaker, and he often speaks of the fear and trembling that fills him each time he approaches the task, even after thirty years in the ministry in the same church. But when he preaches, the word is proclaimed. Truth through personality is never more apparent.

The key to his preparation is his disciplined commitment to a life of prayer. Daily he enters into a quiet place to touch the silent Presence deep within himself, entering into that experience where his life and the presence of God intersect. His sermons leave no doubt that the internal nature of both the inspiration and authority of scripture has been revealed to him as he has listened and prayed.

This man's preaching demonstrates the fact that at its best preaching is an extension of the prayer life of the one who preaches. Prayer is to preaching what planting seeds is to the harvest. The latter cannot exist unless the former is done first.

Again, Phillips Brooks made this point in his Yale lectures when he spoke of the necessary qualities of the preacher:

> I must not dwell upon the first of all the necessary qualities, and yet there is not a moment's doubt that it does stand first of all. It is personal piety, a deep possession in one's own soul of the faith and hope and resolution which he is to offer to his fellow-men for their new life. Nothing but fire kindles fire.[39]

He went on to say that he wished that he could put in some words of new and overwhelming force the old accepted certainty that to live by Christ, to be his, not our own, is the first necessity of the preacher, and "to preach without that is weary and unsatisfying and unprofitable . . . [but] to preach with that is a perpetual privilege and joy."[40]

Prayer is the preparation that is necessary for preaching. Study is a part of the preparation as well. But prayer breathes life into a sermon, because through prayer God breathes life into the one who is preaching. Yet the minister's prayer life cannot be confined to the day of sermon preparation. Instead, prayer needs to be that which undergirds the daily life of the minister. When the minister's life is one of disciplined prayer, sermons are always in germination. The seeds are growing even while the ground is not being tilled. Ministers whose sermons grow up in prayer will find it necessary to carry a notepad all the time in order to keep up with the sermons God is putting inside them.

Letting sermons grow up in prayer also nurtures in the minister courage to preach the message God gives. When ministers preach ideas, the anticipation of controversy can lead them to soften the message or, in some instances, to set it aside altogether. But preaching a message that rises up from within one's self cannot be handled so easily. For the minister knows that he/she is dealing with a word that has been given, not created of the human mind alone. Speaking that word becomes an issue of faithfulness or disobedience, following the Lord or denying that one is a member of his company.

Prayer is the primary source of courage ministers have that will free them to challenge the enculturation of the church. Without prayer the price of the challenge will seem too high, the consequences too heavy to carry. But prayer teaches us truth and truth gives courage. This should be obvious to us. It was Jesus who promised that we would know truth—truth that would set us free (*John 8:31*).

We should note, however, that Jesus said, "If you continue in my word . . .," then we will know the truth that brings freedom. The clergy today would do well to remember this first part of the verse. The lack of biblically based preaching, mentioned earlier, calls us to be more committed to continuing in Jesus' word.

Prayer also brings an additional element to preaching. Through prayer the minister experiences the reality of contextual preaching. That is, prayer leads the minister to a deepened awareness of the pastoral needs of his/her church members. Preaching is always pastoral because it is contextual. It never takes place in a vacuum. It comes out of the life of a specific congregation of people with specific needs. Prayer enables the one who preaches to integrate these concerns into the word he/she receives to preach. Every minister's sermons should tell a great deal about the congregation to whom they are spoken, if the minister understands the nature of preaching. One of the problems of ministry, however, is that for all practical purposes we have allowed pastoral care to be defined in terms of a visitation ministry. While this is part of pastoral care, it is such only when that caring is nurtured by the minister's prayer life. Caring means to stand with people, to live with them in a way that they know one is *for* them and will not leave them to struggle alone. Only prayer in which the lives of the members are held up to God for grace and healing can give authenticity to pastoral visitation. And only in such prayer can the sermon be infused with an overriding pastoral concern.

This aspect of the relationship between preaching and prayer is very important. The Old Testament prophets were who they were because they were pastors first.[41] They loved the people to whom they spoke. Their words of challenge came from the anguish (not anger) they felt for the people. Whatever prophetic word there might be in our preaching cannot be spoken, and surely will not be heard, unless the people to whom we speak know that we care about them. Pastoral care will not guarantee that the congregation will listen to the message. The biblical prophets, and Jesus himself, found no eager audience. But without pastoral care, preaching cannot proclaim the heart of the gospel message about God so loving the world that he sent his son, not to condemn the world, but that the world might be saved through him (*John 3:16-17*).

Emphasizing the centrality of prayer in preaching, however, does not minimize the need for serious study. In chapter 2 we argued for a recovery of the model of the pastor as theologian. Preaching is where the concept will find its fullest expression. Sermons offer the pastor who is a theologian the weekly opportunity to hold up to church members the riches and relevance of the gospel for their lives. Moreover, through preaching, church members learn the value of study for their pastor. When they hear the fruits of the pastor's labor, church members grow in their appreciation of the role study must have in their minister's daily schedule. In this regard, study can be likened to prayer. Both bear good fruit in the sermon when they are practiced in a disciplined fashion. And discipline is the necessary quality in each. Prayer and study cannot be limited to sermon preparation. They have to be the building blocks for one's total ministry.

Summary

Preaching has a vital role to play in breaking the hold that enculturation has on today's church. It must tell the story of *whose* we are as a covenant people and equip us for wise moral/ethical decision-making. But for preaching to fulfill this monumental task, it must grow in both disciplined study and disciplined prayer. In study the minister hears the story of God's love and grace again and again; and in prayer he or she is touched by God's ineffable presence afresh and empowered with confidence to go out and proclaim the message he/she has been given.

5

The Virgin Birth of the Church

This chapter probably should have been first, for it attempts to define the nature of the church, the theological foundation for our challenge to enculturation. The practical steps we have already discussed are central to what must be done in American church life today. But we must also continue to do the theological work that is necessary to keep everything in proper perspective. One of the tendencies of the modern church is to act without giving serious theological reflection to its actions. To a significant extent, this is why church life has become enculturated.

We also need to reaffirm the belief that theology is not the exclusive concern of professional theologians. It is the concern of all Christians. We should not forget that the New Testament was written by people who, with the exception of the apostle Paul, today would be called members of the laity. In my opinion, little in the way of lasting good can come from efforts that do not have sound theology behind them.

Now to the theological task before us. We can begin by saying that one of the first things to be said about the church is that its origins are *divine*. But to say this seems as if we are repeating an age-worn cliche. Yet this may be the most profound statement we can make about the church. It is quite likely that as church members we have lost touch with just how true this statement is, magnifying the tendency to depend more on ourselves and less on God. This in turn has made us even more susceptible to enculturation.

Enculturation is symptomatic of an identity crisis in the church. But it is not simply a matter of not knowing who we are as the church. The real problem is that we do not know *whose* we are. Yet knowing *whose* we are is the only way we can know *who* we are. The church's identity is interwoven with the nature of its *belonging.* Covenant means relationships. Insofar as the church is concerned, we who are members belong to God because we are in a relationship with Jesus Christ. This Christ-relationship has defined *whose* we are, and therefore, *who* we are.

In *The Acts of the Apostles,* Luke provides a graphic description of whose we are as the church. In fact, Luke tells us the story of what can be appropriately called the "virgin birth" of the church, the meaning of which is found in the theological meaning of the Virgin Birth story of Jesus. Luke, of course, is one of two evangelists who includes the Virgin Birth story in his Gospel, Matthew being the other. Unfortunately, the modern church had for the most part overlooked the theological significance of the Virgin Birth stories of Jesus. Instead, we have argued about, and even suffered breaks in Christian fellowship over, the historical basis of these stories.

Part of the reason this has happened lies in the fact that we do not know our church history very well. It comes as a surprise to many church members, for example, to learn that the stories of the Virgin Birth of Jesus have been interpreted as proof both of his divinity and his humanity.[42] St. Augustine (fifth century) is the primary source for use of the Virgin Birth stories as proof of Jesus' divinity. Believing original sin to have been passed on through sexual propagation, Augustine viewed human nature itself as sinful. Anyone born of natural human procreation was infected with the disease of sin. Jesus, the Savior of sinful human beings, obviously could not share in this sinful condition and still be the Savior. Thus, Augustine understood the conception by the Holy Spirit as the clear sign that Jesus did not share in the human condition. He was divine because of the Holy Spirit conception. Therefore, he was sinless.

Before Augustine we find evidence that Christians viewed the Virgin Birth of Jesus from an entirely different perspective. Ignatius of Antioch, for example, in the second century interpreted the stories as proof of Jesus' genuine humanity. His understanding of the Virgin Birth countered what Ignatius viewed as the distortions of the Docetists, who taught that Jesus was not truly human. Even though conception was by the Holy Spirit, Ignatius believed, the fact that Jesus was born of a woman's womb left no question that he was fully human.

What both of these examples indicate is that Christians have not understood the Virgin Birth stories in the same way and that they have been viewed as proof of both Jesus' divinity and his humanity. Moreover, from a theological point of view, both Ignatius and Augustine were correct. The central affirmation of the Christian faith has been and remains that Jesus was both human and divine. To explain how this was so is to attempt to explain the miracle of all miracles. And when miracles are explained, the result is that they are simply explained away. There seems to be no evidence that the Gospel writers were seeking to explain the nature of Jesus' being when they recorded the Virgin Birth narratives. Their concern was at another point altogether. For example, New Testament scholar Charles Talbert says that by including the Virgin Birth story in his Gospel, Luke was declaring:

> The greatness of Jesus' life was not a human achievement,
> but the result of divine intervention. Jesus' career was not
> the result of the perfection of human striving and effort;
> only God could produce a life like his. Jesus was God's
> act.[43]

The emphasis here should be on the statement, "Jesus was God's act." This is the theological meaning of the Virgin Birth. Jesus was the act of God. That's the point! If we miss this, we miss it all. When Luke's original readers read what he wrote, they would not have missed it. They would have recognized that the gospel about Jesus was not going to be about a great man who did good things for others. They would have known, instead, that they were about to read the story of a life in which God was involved, a life which glorified God because it was a life God willed into existence.

The Church as God's Act

Now, it is this understanding of the Virgin Birth of Jesus that forms the basis for what we are saying about the church. What

Luke says about the birth of Jesus, he also says about the birth of the church. That is, as Jesus was the act of God, so is the church. The description he gives us of the experience of the disciples on Pentecost (*Acts 2*) needs to be understood as functioning theologically in the same way for the church as the Virgin Birth narratives function for Jesus' birth. Both Jesus and the church are to be seen as God's act and not the result of human striving or achievement. The church is the result of divine intervention, as is its Lord. Therefore, the ministry of the church is not powered by the genius of dedicated men and women. Rather, the church was born of God and survives only by the continued breath of God breathing life into it. Its life came by his Spirit, and will continue by it and by no other means. Therefore, the church belongs to God. He is *whose* we are.

However, the divine origin of the church Luke describes is not simply a theological concept. Rather than intellectual statements of faith, the Gospels are *confessions of faith*. Luke was conceptualizing what he had already experienced to be true. In his personal encounter with the raised Christ, Luke had come to know the power of God at work in the church's life. This is because Christianity is experiential. In the deepest sense the church is not a religion, although beliefs and practices are important elements of church life. Rather, Christianity is a relationship. This is what the divine origin of the church means. The God of our faith is not one who is to be known about. He is one to be known! To belong to God means living in relationship to him.

Essential to breaking out of cultural bondage is recognizing that this is the nature of our faith. The seeds of enculturation find fertile ground in a faith that has become a religion that is bound up in beliefs and ceremony. Perhaps no one has made this point so powerfully as the nineteenth-century Russian novelist Dostoyevsky, in his book *The Brothers Karamazov*. Dostoyevsky describes the "Grand Inquisitor," a cardinal of the church of Spain around the time of the Spanish Inquisition of the 1500s, meeting Christ who has returned to earth and appears in Seville. Christ came softly, unobserved, says Dostoyevsky, yet every one recognized him. The common people, the tortured, the suffering, and those sunk in iniquity were all irresistibly drawn to him. And he loved them. They felt the warmth of his gentle smile of infinite compassion. At one point he raises a little girl out of a coffin as she is being carried to her burial.

The cardinal, the Grand Inquisitor, passes the cathedral at the moment of the miracle and sees what has happened. Immediately he summons the guards to arrest the Christ, and they take him away to prison. Later the old cardinal quizzes the Christ about his return to earth. The cardinal is angry about the return. He tells the Christ he has no right to add anything to what he has already said. Besides, the church has its beliefs and holy observances. Christ's return, says the Grand Inquisitor, is only a hindrance to church life. He is not needed. And after a long interrogation, during which the Christ remains characteristically silent, the Grand Inquisitor simply sends him away with the words: "Go, and come no more . . . come not at all, never, never!"[44] And the Christ leaves.

Dostoyevsky, of course, wrote the story as a severe criticism of the church of his own day. Whether or not he was somewhat strident in his criticism remains an open question, but the warning in the story is vitally important to the spiritual health of the church. Whenever Christianity becomes intractably wrapped up in beliefs and practices, it moves away from the relationship with Christ that provides the source and validity of its life.

As church members we need to realize that enculturation feeds on religion *about* God, but is threatened by a relationship *with* God. This is why we must not substitute belief in the resurrection for the relationship with the raised Christ that God has made possible. Our culture accommodates religion about God because such religion never challenges the idolatry that culture represents and perpetuates. But people who encounter the presence of God know the truth about culture. They recognize cultural pharoahs as power brokers who refuse to acknowledge their own limits and ignore the One to whom they are ultimately accountable.

If we are enculturated as church members today, it is because we have allowed religiosity to diminish our sense of the presence of Christ. This means that the first step toward freedom is once again to open our lives to experiencing his presence. We must discover anew that the power of the gospel is not the fact that Jesus lived but that he *lives;* not that we can talk about him, but that we can *know* him. If this cannot happen to us, then our faith is null and void, as Paul stated bluntly in *1 Corinthians 15:13-14:* "But if there is no resurrection of the dead, then Christ has not been raised; if Christ has not been raised, then our preaching is in vain and your faith is in vain."

The boldness of Paul's words can be understood only if we realize that he was talking about the resurrection based upon his own experience, much as Luke described the divine origins of the church based upon his experience with Christ. Paul did not decide to believe Jesus was the Christ after rethinking his original position. Rather, his life was turned around because he experienced the truth of Christ's resurrection. His belief that Jesus was the Christ was the natural extension of meeting the raised Lord. So powerful was the presence of Christ in Paul's life thereafter that he was later to describe what happened by saying: "I have been crucified with Christ; it is no longer I who live, but Christ who lives in me" (*Galatians 2:20*).

That Paul understood faith as experiential is also seen in his statement in *2 Corinthians 5:19:*

> . . . in Christ God was reconciling the world to himself,
> not counting their trespasses against them, and entrusting
> to us the message of reconciliation.

The full power of this verse is recognized when we note that the literal Greek for the translation "entrusting to us" means "to put or place inside us." From this we can see that the gospel message is something we experience. It is proclaimed only after it has become a part of our inward being. Further, the fact that this can happen to us rests on the reality of the presence of the raised Christ.

Yet in spite of what we are saying about the New Testament witness to experiential faith, it is not the kind of experience many of us can identify with much specificity. It seems to border on the kind of religious emotionalism that makes us uncomfortable and of which we are usually very skeptical.

But this is not what we are trying to describe. While I believe emotions are a legitimate part of faith, I am not suggesting that experiential faith is the kind that leads us to raise our hands in public worship or go off on lay witness teams to tell others what

Jesus has done for us. These may be expressions of genuine faith experiences, but there are others that are no less real, even if less obvious in any outward display of emotionalism.

For example, Martin Luther King, Jr. once described an encounter with the presence of God, showing that the faith that sustained him in his struggle for racial justice was experiential. In a sermon preached at Ebenezer Baptist Church in Atlanta, he told of being overcome by fear in the early days of the civil rights struggle and wanting to get out while he still could. It was during the Montgomery bus boycott, when Dr. King was a young man who had been thrust into the leadership of the movement. Late one night after a particularly stressful day, he received a threatening phone call. The voice on the other end said, "Listen, nigger, by this time next week you'll wish you never came to Montgomery."

He had received calls like this one before, each time taking them in stride. But this one affected him more than usual. He became filled with fear. He couldn't go back to sleep. He got up, paced the floor for a long time, and finally went into the kitchen and fixed himself a pot of coffee. He was ready to give up, but did not want to appear cowardly. Finally he placed his head in his hands and began to pray, perhaps as he had never prayed before. This is how he described what happened in his praying:

> At that moment I experienced the presence of the Divine as I had never before experienced him. It seemed as though I could hear the quiet assurance of an inner voice, saying, "Stand up for righteousness, stand up for truth. God will be at your side forever." Almost at once my fears began to pass from me. My uncertainty disappeared. I was ready to face anything. The outer situation remained the same, but God had given me inner calm.

Only a few nights later the King home was bombed. But he said he accepted it calmly because of his experience with the presence of God only a few nights before.

What Dr. King described was being enveloped by the presence of God which revealed itself through a deep inner feeling of security and peace. His strength and will to go on were renewed, and he knew that God had ministered to him that night.

Dr. King's experience testifies that God can be as real to us today as he was to the people of the Bible. His experience also reminds us that when we go through periods of doubt and fear, and experience a renewal of our inner security and strength, then we can be assured that we have been in the presence of the Lord.

St. Bernard of Clairvaux

St. Bernard of Clairvaux, a twelfth-century monk, described love's development in the Christian's life in a way that may be helpful to us in understanding what experiential faith means.[46]

Bernard believed that human love matures under the guidance of the Spirit of God. He identified particular stages of love's development. The first stage is love of self for self's sake. Bernard thought this was where love started. Because we are flesh and blood, born of the desire of the flesh, our first capacity to love is basically selfish: the love of self for self's sake.

But Bernard also believed that, because of faith, we could move from this elementary level of love to loving God. Yet even this love was thought to be selfish. Thus, he called it the stage of loving God for self's sake.

From this stage, Bernard suggested, we can move to a higher level of love. As our capacity to love matures in the Spirit, we move to the level he described as loving God for God's sake. Having learned from stage two something of the satisfaction and fulfillment of loving God, albeit through self-centered love, we can love God for God's sake as the next logical step. Here the Christian loves God with a God-centered love, seeking to praise and please God without expecting something in return.

This stage of loving God for God's sake would seem to be the highest level we could reach. But Bernard surprises us. He said there was yet another level of love's maturity in the Spirit. This is the level of loving one's self for God's sake. This is the highest level of love. Bernard described the process by which this level is reached:

When the good and faithful servant shall have been brought into the joy of his Lord and becomes inebriated with the fulness of the house of God.[47]

Bernard doubted whether anyone had ever reached this level in earthly life. Perhaps he was correct—then and now. But his stages of spiritual maturity do suggest a way for us to monitor our own spiritual growth. It seems reasonable to suppose that, the closer we move to loving ourselves for God's sake, the more secure we become inwardly. Yet even the third level Bernard identified, that of loving God for God's sake, would seem to form a basis for inward security. The less selfish we become in our capacity to love, the greater our willingness to remain faithful in our covenant relationship with God, and the more determined we will be to please God rather than people.

The genius of Bernard was in linking love for God and love for self. This is especially important for those of us in the church today. Self-denial, important as this may be in submission to God's will, has come to mean something close to self-hatred; at the least, self-effacement. Many of us think that self-love cannot rise above selfishness. It took the insight of a Bernard of Clairvaux to show us that the more excellent way of love (*2 Corinthians 13*) includes one's self. The capacity to love God, others, and one's self is the same love in each instance; only the channel is different. At the same time, *not* to channel our love in any of these ways affects loving in the other relationships.

We may find ourselves moving from one stage of love to another at different times in our lives. But St. Bernard's description does suggest a practical way for us to measure the maturity of our love. And the closer we move toward the fourth stage, the more we can trust that we are living deeper and deeper into God's Presence.

Christ Among Marginal People

We have already underscored the need for churches in America to become identified with the marginal people of our society: the poor, the hungry, the sick, the imprisoned, the forgotten. But what we have not said is that, according to Jesus himself, the seeds of experiential faith are in this kind of identification. In order to understand what he was saying, we need first to recognize the fact that most of us in the church think of helping marginal people as an obligation. It is a commandment to follow. In fact, many church members view the social dimensions of ministry almost as burdens. Not that some of us do not want to do them. Rather, it is a matter of social ministries being difficult, requiring time, money, and energy.

The problem is that we have overlooked two very important dimensions of helping marginal people. One is the fact that social ministries are something we cannot *not* do, if we truly know Christ. Earlier we mentioned that Paul said God has "put inside" us the message of reconciliation, meaning that reconciliation is a part of our makeup as Christians. Before we do the ministry of reconciliation, God first makes us reconcilers through Christ.

This being the case, ministry among marginal people (which is reconciliation) is a natural by-product of *whose we are* and *what we have become* as Christians. Not to do this ministry would be like not breathing. The extent to which we experience Christ's presence in becoming reconcilers will determine the degree to which our social ministry is either a joy or a burden.

Enculturation, of course, works against our becoming reconcilers. It tempts us to view reconciliation as a commandment precisely because it wants us to think of helping others as a burden. The tragedy is that enculturation has been effective in this regard. As church members we have externalized social ministries to the point where they seldom have roots in the life of the Spirit, causing us to lose patience quickly and to become discouraged easily. This is why church members are prone to give money for someone else to do social ministries rather than to seek to become involved themselves. Herein is why we must begin to look for Christ's presence among those we are helping. The less real Christ's presence is, as we minister to marginal people, the more difficult it will be for us to do these ministries.

The second dimension of helping these people is inextricably related to the first one. This dimension is recognizing that marginal people have much to give to us. No one in contemporary church life has been a more effective voice in stating what marginal people have to give us than Mother Theresa of Calcutta. This remarkable saint of the church has called upon

Christians to realize that such people do not need our pity; they need our respect. She calls them a great people whose capacity to give love and not just receive it has not been recognized. In her acceptance speech for the Nobel Peace Prize, Mother Theresa said:

> Our poor people are great people, a very lovable people. They don't need our pity and sympathy. They need our understanding love and they need our respect. We need to tell the poor that they are somebody to us, that they, too, have been created by the same loving hand of God, to love and be loved.[48]

We must be careful not to allow enculturation to cause us to hear Mother Theresa's words as a challenge to help marginal people while missing her point that they have much to give to us. As church members we must resist influences that would have us believe the poor are lazy and "good-for-nothing," living as parasites off the hard work of other people.

When we have this image of marginal people, we do not think of them as having anything to give. We see them as takers, not givers. But Mother Theresa is teaching us this is not true. She describes experiences such as staying up all night with a dying woman who had been found on the street, her feet eaten off by rats. As she ministered, the woman said to her, "Thank you." Those words, Mother Theresa recalled, gave her more than she had given to the dying woman.

The irony is that we should not be surprised to know marginal people have much to give us. Jesus told us that he would be among them. In feeding, clothing, and visiting them we would, he said, find him (*Matthew 25:31-46*). That is why they have so much to give us. Christ is there with them. They reveal him to us.[49] What a paradox! We go to them because Christ has filled us with reconciliation, but when we get there we discover that he is already among them. In being with marginal people we experience the presence of Christ which then strengthens our own commitment to be reconcilers.

All of this suggests that one of the important ways we grow in our relationship with Christ is knowing personally the marginal people of our communities. We must get beyond the issues and get to know them personally. Christ's presence cannot be found in an issue. It is found only in people. The challenge church members face is to move out of the church building, where issues are discussed and debated, and to go to the inner city, where these people can be found. We need to learn their names and addresses. We need to hear what they are thinking and feeling.

At our college we have developed a program which brings students together with marginal people in our city as a part of their growth in Christian discipleship. Through the years we have seen the difference it makes in these students' lives when we stop talking about issues like poverty and start getting to know marginal people on a personal basis. The difference is like night and day. We have been doing this long enough now to see that meeting marginal people has had a renewing effect on many of these students because they have experienced the presence of Christ among these people. It may not always happen, but Christ has promised us that it can happen if we are open to it.

Christ can be found among all kinds of people. But he has promised us that he can be found among marginal people. Such people are all around us. In ministering to them, we can expect to experience the presence of the Lord of the church. He has assured us he would meet us there.

Summary

What we have said in this chapter is that the church was born from an act of God. It is not simply a human institution functioning in modern society. It is a divine institution, meaning that faith is not simply a matter of beliefs; it is an experience of the presence of the raised Christ.

This experience of faith is the foundation for limiting the influence of enculturation in the church. Each time the presence of Christ is experienced, we deepen our commitment to belonging to God. Thus, being faithful to his will becomes more important to us than cultural acceptance or success. If the practical steps we must take in our battle against enculturation are severed from experiential faith, there is little chance we will take them. If we do not know *whose* we are, as the church, we will never know *who* we are, leaving us confused and easy prey for cultural values that claim our loyalty.

Conclusion

My concern in this discussion has been two-fold: One, that as church members we recognize our enculturation; two, that we take the steps necessary to reestablish our relationship to God as his covenant people.

The hope that we can actually do both of these is undergirded by the amazing faith that God has in us. It is true enough that our life as a covenant community depends on our faith in God. For us Christians, our personal relationship to Christ is the way in which this faith is actualized. For us, to know Christ is to know God and to be empowered by him to do his will.

Yet the biblical tradition reminds us that God's gracious gifts of his presence and salvation do not leave us with no role to play in this covenant relationship. We normally describe our role in terms of obedience. While obedience is an appropriate term, the biblical witness enlivens it with the concept of "blessing ourselves." Because of God's covenant with us, we have the opportunity to bless ourselves.

In the book of *Genesis,* God makes a promise to Abraham and Sarah. The promise is for a future. God tells them he will make of them a great nation and that he will bless them and make their name great (*12:1-3*). As the text stands, this promise is startling.[50] It comes as a complete surprise because it immediately follows the revelation that Sarah is barren! (*11:30*). She has no child and no hope of having one. Sarah and Abraham stand before an empty future, before no future. Their line will end with their deaths, and they are helpless to change anything about that fact.

But then the promise is given. God tells them they will have a future. They will become a great nation and will be blessed. While they look to a future with no descendants, God promises them they will have many. What is more, they will become a blessing to all the nations. Through them all the families of the earth will bless themselves! (*12:3*).

This promise of God became a tangible reality in the birth of Isaac, Jacob, and Joseph. Later, it was awakened again in the Sinai covenant and reaffirmed in Joshua's Shechem covenant renewal ceremony. We are the heirs of that promise because we are *b'nai b'rith,* children of covenant. Through Jesus Christ, God has given us the opportunity to bless ourselves. Because Abraham and Sarah are our spiritual ancestors, we stand under their blessing and can bless ourselves.

The church today is called to be children of covenant. We have said that it does not go far enough to say that we are the people of God. We are also the people of covenant. By honoring this covenant relationship, we have the opportunity to witness to God's promise that all the families of the earth can bless themselves. This is why covenant renewal is such a critical need in the church. Enculturation is stripping us of the will to be a faithful covenant partner and thus is destroying our witness to the promise of blessing.

Perhaps it is in the loss of will that our real sin lies. Scripture tells us that Christ died for us while we were yet sinners (*Romans 5:8*). This means humankind has, and will always stand in need of, God's grace for salvation. Sin is a reality from which we shall now be free in this life. But the will to do God's will is within our power, even if the flesh is weak (*Romans 7:15-19*). Enculturation is weakening the will to be a faithful covenant partner.

Every generation has probably thought that its own hour was late. But there does seem to be an urgency about today that did not exist in the past. This modern generation has, for the first time, developed the power to destroy civilization as we know it, perhaps even life on this planet. For the church to do business as usual, believing there is no serious ailment infecting church life today, is tantamount to Nero fiddling while Rome burned. Enculturation is eroding our perception of the forces of evil at work in the world that are leading nations to ultimate destruction; forces of evil which are the ultimate denial of the sovereignty of God.

It is not pessimism to want church members to face the problem of enculturation. On the contrary, it is a firm belief that the covenant can be renewed, which in turn can empower us to witness to life against the forces of death, that drives us to call Christ's church to covenant renewal. The church can be a blessing to the nations leading all the families of the earth to bless themselves. As a faithful covenant partner, the church, through its words *and* deeds, declares to the world that evil will *not* win the day, and that God is about his creative work once again, bringing order out of the present chaos so that one day we will see

... a new heaven and a new earth; for the first heaven and the first earth had passed away ...

and hear

... a loud voice from the throne saying, "Behold, the dwelling of God is with men [people]. He will dwell with them, and they shall be his people and God himself will be with them; he will wipe away every tear from their eyes, and death shall be no more, neither shall there be mourning nor crying nor pain any more, for the former things have passed away (*Revelation 21:1, 3-4*).

As children of the covenant, may we be witnesses in the world that these words are trustworthy and true (*21:6*).

Appendix

This service is offered as a guide to congregations in planning an annual covenant renewal service. It will need to be adapted to the particular personality of individual congregations. But the theme and flow of the service should be retained. Each part (order, prayers, covenant, scripture, hymns, etc.) has been carefully thought through. Any change should be consistent with the purpose of the service.

A collection of small smooth stones (or some other appropriate covenant symbol) should be available so that each worshiper may bring one into the sanctuary at the beginning of worship.

Covenant Renewal Service

The Prelude

The Processional Hymn
"All People That on Earth Do Dwell"
Tune: Old Hundredth

The Call to Worship
Leader: Spirit of God, descend upon our hearts.
People: Come alive in us, awaken us.
Leader: Illumine us, encourage us.
People: Empower us, guide us.
All: Spirit of God, possess our hearts. Spirit of Joy, express yourself through us. Renew us, fill us, use us today, tomorrow, always, forever.

The Invocation (by minister or worship leader; provided here, but does not necessarily have to be printed in the bulletin)

O Lord, when we pause to reflect on who we are—creatures made by the Creator, children of a loving Father, finite beings connected to the Infinite, sinners redeemed by God's own Son, human beings loved by the Almighty God—there is only one appropriate response—to bow down and worship you.

Yet a submissive attitude does not come easy for us. We are sophisticated achievers who have split the atom, put men on the moon, and broken the genetic code. It is hard for us to acknowledge dependency in our lives.

Yet because we are also people of faith who believe we are created in your image, and because we know that it is you who seeks, initiates, and desires to maintain fellowship with us—we feel called to respond.

Help us to respond with our lives, accepting your unfathomable mercy and love, pledging who we are and what we have been given to enhancing the human condition with compassionate acts and with responsible stewardship of our home, the Earth. Amen.

The Statement of Welcome and Purpose (to be read by Worship Leader)

We believe that the God of Israel and of Jesus is the Creator and Sustainer of all life. As children of covenant, we come here acknowledging his sovereignty over our lives and over this congregation of believers. And we come to renew our commitment to seek his will in the coming year. As we renew our covenant today, we proclaim Jesus the Christ as Savior and Lord. It is through him that we can know whose we are and what we are to do as the church.

We believe there is power in a faith community which enables the members to do together what they cannot do alone.

Today we come pledging to make our deeds consistent with our words and our living consistent with our believing.

The Hymn of Affirmation
"Be Thou My Vision" or *Anthem* here
Tune: Slane

The Scripture Readings (choose from the list of suggested readings)
Jeremiah 32:36-41
Psalm 111
Mark 8:34—9:1
Luke 24:36-51
John 13:31-36
Romans 12
Galatians 3:23-29
Ephesians 4:1-13
Hebrews 10:19-25
Revelation 21:1-5

The Sermon

The Covenant Renewal
Silence (2 to 3 minutes, introduced by Worship Leader)

Scripture Reading: Joshua 24:14-18; Matthew 5:1-16

The Statement of Covenant (unison)
In Jesus Christ, God has called us to be members of the company of his covenant people, not because we are worthy of this call, but because of God's love and mercy freely given to us. Yet we know that God's covenant of grace challenges us to be a faithful people, challenges us to be responsible in the freedom we enjoy under his mercy.

We come to this moment as an act of choosing this day whom we will serve. We will serve the God of Abraham and Sarah, Isaac and Rebekah, Jacob and Rachel, the God of Moses and David, the God of our Lord. In this choice we reject any claims the gods of culture make upon us, pledging that in the next year we will seek to be a congregation of covenant people whose life and ministry unequivocally witness to the name we claim as the church of Jesus Christ.

We pledge to support one another in prayer and presence, and to support our common ministry in the exercising of gifts and the giving of a portion of our income. In making this choice we celebrate the life together that God has given to us in Christ.

(To be followed by the Apostles' Creed or denominational statement of faith, where appropriate)

The Eucharist
The Offering
The Gloria Patri
The Eucharistic Prayer
The Sharing

The Dedication of the Covenant Symbol
(Minister reads Joshua 4:1-7 as congregation stands, each person holding a stone as they sing and pray the benediction.)

The Hymn of Dedication
"Take My Life and Let it Be"
Tune: Vienna

The Prayer of Benediction (in unison)
Almighty God, we have come to this service of worship truly grateful for our past year together. Thank you for each time we have gathered to celebrate in your name. Thank you for the increased good, growth, and unfolding this year has brought to us.

In the days and weeks ahead, give us faith to believe
. . . that if we seek your kingdom first, you will supply all our lesser needs.
. . . that if we put trust in you, we can participate in your creative work among peoples.
. . . that each of us has a special gift to exercise for the betterment of others.
. . . that each of us has been endowed by you with immeasurable worth.

With you in our hearts, O God, the journey of our lives is always forward and progressive. So bless us, Lord, as we journey. And help us realize that journeying is more than reaching destinations. Journeying is the celebration of life along the way as we accept your will as our own. Amen.

The Postlude

(Each person keeps the stone, or other symbol, for the next year as a covenant reminder.)

Notes

1. One example is my own denomination. At its September 1983 General Assembly, two resolutions calling for evangelism as the priority of the church were passed. Other denominations have either already developed new programs or are being pressured by clergy and laity to do so.

2. Key-73, the major evangelistic effort launched in 1973, is a case in point. The program was sponsored by the Billy Graham Association, with most major Protestant denominations participating. It was intended to evangelize America and strengthen local churches. Yet during the last ten years America has, if anything, grown more secular, and churches have declined.

3. H. Richard Niebuhr defines culture as "the 'artificial,' secondary environment which man superimposes on the natural. It is comprised of language, habits, ideas, beliefs, customs, social organization, inherited artifacts, technical processes, and values." (*Christ and Culture,* Harper & Row, p. 32.) Niebuhr's historical analysis of the tensions among Christ, Christianity, and culture is a classic.

4. He used these terms in a lecture on the American civilization and its future delivered in September 1983, at Lynchburg College, Lynchburg, Virginia.

5. The 1984 annual report on poverty of the U.S. Census Bureau states that in 1983 the national poverty rate remained at its highest level in eighteen years. The *Economic Opportunity Report,* October 24, 1983, made a similar report, with an additional study indicating that the degree of poverty has also increased, which means the poor are getting poorer. Also, the

Harvard School of Public Health study recently indicated that infant mortality increased by nearly 50 percent in one year in some of Boston's poorest neighborhoods, while infant deaths were declining nationwide (AP, *The Daily Advance,* Lynchburg, Virginia, Wednesday, July 25, 1984). On a worldwide scale, the United Nations Children's Emergency Fund (UNICEF) estimates that 40,000 children die daily from hunger and its related diseases.

6. This is similar to what Dietrich Bonhoeffer called "costless grace" in his book *The Cost of Discipleship.*

7. This is what happened to Dr. Eberhard Bethge, a close friend and associate of Bonhoeffer's, when he visited this church while serving as scholar-in-residence at Lynchburg College in the fall of 1981. Disturbed by the flag and pin, Dr. Bethge made mention of it in several lectures, each time asking the people present, "Do you know what happens when these two are put together? This one always wins" (pointing to the flag).

8. Another example of Americanizing the gospel was a sermon preached by James Kennedy of Coral Ridge Ministries, Florida, on November 28, 1982. In his sermon Kennedy stated that being a good Christian meant being a good American, and being a good American meant being a good Christian. A letter was written asking him to explain his views, but no reply was received.

9. See my book *Living out God's Love* (Valley Forge: Judson Press, 1981); also, Elizabeth O'Connor's books *Call to Commitment* and *Journey Inward, Journey Outward;* and Elton Trueblood's *The Company of the Committed* and *The Incendiary Fellowship.*

10. The Shechem narratives clearly stand in the Sinai Covenant tradition. In addition, it is likely that at Shechem Joshua instituted the twelve-tribe confederacy which lasted to the period of the judges. See Martin Noth's *The History of Israel,* Second edition (New York: Harper & Row, 1960), pp. 89-93.

11. For further discussion of this point, see Bernhard Anderson's *Understanding the Old Testament,* Third edition (New Jersey: Prentice-Hall, Inc., 1957), pp. 128-129.

12. For an excellent discussion of the biblical roots of the concept of "the alternative community," see Walter Brueggemann's *The Prophetic Imagination* (Philadelphia: Fortress Press, 1978), p. 11.

13. Hobart Mowrer, *The Crisis in Psychiatry and Religion* (Princeton: D. Van Nostrand Co., Inc.), p. 139.

14. *Ibid.,* p. 141.

15. Regarding this issue, we have confined ourselves to the local congregation. It may be necessary for such church institutions as colleges and hospitals to build endowments, but local congregations do not require endowments for accreditation or survivability. At the same time, we would speak a word of caution against denominational offices building endowments. While the issue at this level is more complex than on the congregational level, building endowments for general church purposes may create more problems than they solve. Certainly, denominational investments in corporate America have compromised the church's prophetic voice on national and global moral issues. Some examples are those of holding investments in companies that do business with South Africa's apartheid government and companies that profit from the nuclear arms race.

16. A provocative study of the radical nature of conversion is Jim Wallis' *The Call to Conversion* (San Francisco: Harper & Row, 1983).

17. Theological education in America in recent years has seen the need to recover this model for its curriculum. See Edward Farley's *Theologia: The Fragmentation and Unity of Theological Education* (Philadelphia: Fortress Press, 1983).

18. Roy Oswald, *Clergy Stress: A Survival Kit for Church Professionals* (Washington, DC: The Alban Institute).

19. Robert K. Greenleaf describes the power of the servant leader concept in his essay, *The Servant As Leader* (Cambridge: Center for Applied Studies, 1970).

20. See Robert N. Bellah's classic essay on "Civil Religion in America" in *Beyond Belief* (New York: Harper and Row, 1970), pp. 168-189. This first appeared in *Daedalus,* Winter 1967.

21. James A. Sanders says that the so-called prophets "never 'denied' that God was the God of Israel who had elected Israel and redeemed them from slavery in Egypt . . . and/or had chosen David and established his throne and city . . . But in addition to affirming God as redeemer and sustainer, the true prophets stressed that God was also creator of all peoples of all the earth." See his essay, "Hermeneutics in True and False Prophecy" in

Canon and Authority, ed. by George W. Coats and Burke O. Long (Philadelphia: Fortress Press, 1977), p. 37.

22. Some scholars believe the emphasis in this passage was originally intended to be the name "Jesus." The writer, they say, wanted his readers to believe that Jesus of Nazareth was the Christ of faith. Should this be the case, it does not alter the emphasis we are making.

23. See Lou H. Silberman's essay, "Listening to the Text," *Journal of Biblical Literature* (Vol. 102, No. 1, March, 1983).

24. To understand the function of story in the development of the biblical canon, see James A. Sanders, *Torah and Canon* (Philadelphia: Fortress Press, 1972). See also his essay, "Adaptable For Life: The Nature and Function of Canon" in *Magnailia Dei: The Mighty Acts of God,* ed. by Cross, Learke, and Miller (Garden City: Doubleday, 1976), pp. 531-60. In *The Creative Word: Canon as a Model for Biblical Education* (Philadelphia: Fortress Press, 1982), Brueggemann describes the use of story as a hermeneutical tool for the church's educational ministry.

25. See chapter 4 of Brueggemann's *The Creative Word* for an in-depth discussion of the role of the wisdom tradition in the biblical canon and its implications for today.

26. This methodology for moral/ethical decision-making is discussed in detail by Brevard Childs in *Biblical Theology in Crisis* (Philadelphia: Fortress Press, 1970), chapter 7.

27. *Ibid.,* p. 130.

28. There is no consensus among scholars as to the specific customs referred to in this passage. They may have been related to the forbidden practice of Christian proselytizing of Gentiles.

29. Raymond E. Brown, *The Gospel According To John Thirteen—Twenty-One, Anchor Bible, Vol. 29A (Garden City: Doubleday and Co., Inc., 1970), pp. 611-614; 636-648.*

30. *Ibid.*

31. In this chapter, we have not attempted to exhaust the possibilities for revitalizing the church's educational ministry in the congregation. That is a task for those who specialize in the field. Our goal has been more modest in that we have simply advocated that education in the church should nurture members in covenant commitment to Christ that is rooted in experiential faith and have suggested some ways of doing this.

32. Helmut Thielicke, The Trouble with the Church: A Call

for Renewal, tr. and ed. by John W. Doberstein (New York: Harper & Row, 1965).

33. James D. Smart says of the interpretative context: "It is obvious . . . that every man, scholar and layman alike, reads Scripture in an interpretative context. The meaning that seems to us to come directly from the words upon the page is actually an interpretation, the result of an instantaneous and unconscious process by which the words on the page receive specific meanings in our minds . . . Every apprehension of the text and every statement of its meaning is an interpretation and, however adequate—by it expresses the content of the text, it dare not ever be equated with the text itself." *The Strange Silence of the Bible in the Church* (Philadelphia: the Westminster Press, 1970), pp. 53-54.

34. Fred C. Craddock, *As One Without Authority: Essays on Inductive Preaching* (Enid: Phillips University Press, 1971). Craddock argues that preaching that uses the methodology of inductive reasoning is an effective means of coping with the pulpit's lack of authority in modern society, as well as being consistent with Jesus' own use of parables. See also his book, *Overhearing the Gospel* (Nashville: Abingdon, 1978).

35. *The Torah: A Modern Commentary* (New York: The Union of American Hebrew Congregations, 1981), p. xix.

36. Childs, *Biblical Theology in Crisis,* p. 104.

37. Phillips Brooks, *On Preaching* (New York: The Seabury Press, 1964), p. 14.

38. *Ibid.,* p. 5.

39. *Ibid.,* p. 38.

40. *Ibid.,* p. 38-39.

41. See Abraham Heschel's classic work, *The Prophets: An Introduction* (New York: Harper Torchbooks, 1962) to understand what manner of man the prophet was.

42. Charles Talbert, *Reading Luke* (New York: Crossroad, 1982), p. 21.

43. *Ibid.*

44. Dostoyevsky, *The Brothers Karamazov,* tr. by Constance Garnett (New York: Modern Library, Random House), p. 272.

45. Martin Luther King, Jr., *Strength to Love* (New York: Pocket Books, 1964), pp. 131-2.

46. St. Bernard of Clairvaux, *Selected Letters,* translation and

introduction by the Reverend Bruno Scott James (Chicago: Henry Regency Co., 1953), p. 54.

47. *Ibid.,* p. 54.

48. *The New York Times,* December 11, 1979.

49. In a speech before the Urban Industrial Mission Conference in Tokyo in 1975, German theologian Jurgen Moltmann addressed the topic, "Hope in the Struggle of the People." He noted that *Matthew 25* is usually understood as a reference for Christian ethics, as the works of charity. Moltmann argued, however, that such a reading does not go far enough: "Matthew 25 does not make the poor 'objects' of Christian charity works but 'subjects' of the messianic kingdom, namely, brothers and sisters of Christ." He went on to ask: "Where is the true church? It is where Christ is. Christ is present in the mission of the believers *and* the suffering of the least of these." Moltmann suggested that Christians must learn that before we go to the "least of these" Christ is already there: "They are the brothers of Christ, the brothers of the world Judge ('whoever visits them, visits me')" (Reprinted in the March 21, 1977 issue of *Christianity and Crisis,* by permission of the *Andover Newton Quarterly*).

50. Walter Brueggemann, *Genesis* (Interpretation Commentary. Atlanta: John Knox Press, 1982), p. 116.